T0299368

Pricing Non-marketed Goods using Distance Functions

World Scientific–Now Publishers Series in Business

ISSN: 2251-3442

The World Scientific–Now Publishers Series in Business publishes advanced textbooks, research monographs, and edited volumes on a variety of topics in business studies including accounting, entrepreneurship, finance, management, marketing, operations, and strategy. The Series includes both applied and theoretical topics that present current research and represent the state-of-the-art work in their respective fields. Contributed by academic scholars from academic and research institutions worldwide, books published under this Series will be of interest to researchers, doctoral students, and technical professionals.

Published:

Vol. 16 *Pricing Non-marketed Goods using Distance Functions*
by Dimitris Margaritis, Rolf Färe and Shawna Grosskopf

Vol. 15 *Innovative Federal Reserve Policies During the Great Financial Crisis*
edited by Douglas D. Evanoff, George G. Kaufman and A. G. Malliaris

Vol. 14 *Marketing Manipulation: A Consumer's Survival Manual*
by Michael Kamins

Vol. 13 *Project Risk Analysis Made Ridiculously Simple*
by Lev Virine and Michael Trumper

Vol. 12 *Real Options in Energy and Commodity Markets*
edited by Nicola Secomandi

Forthcoming:

Marketing for Economists and Life Scientists: Viewing Marketing Tools as Informative and Risk Reduction/Demand Enhancing
by Amir Heiman and David Zilberman

The complete list of titles in the series can be found at
https://www.worldscientific.com/series/ws-npsb

(Continued at the end of the book)

World Scientific – Now Publishers Series in Business: **Vol. 16**

Pricing Non-marketed Goods using Distance Functions

Rolf Färe
Oregon State University, USA

Shawna Grosskopf
Oregon State University, USA

Dimitris Margaritis
University of Auckland, New Zealand

In collaboration with:
R. Sickles, C. J. Shang, W. L. Weber, and M. Hasannasab

Published by

World Scientific Publishing Co. Pte. Ltd.
5 Toh Tuck Link, Singapore 596224
USA office: 27 Warren Street, Suite 401-402, Hackensack, NJ 07601
UK office: 57 Shelton Street, Covent Garden, London WC2H 9HE

and

now publishers Inc.
PO Box 1024
Hanover, MA 02339
USA

Library of Congress Cataloging-in-Publication Data
Names: Margaritis, Dimitris, author. | Färe, Rolf, 1942– author. |Grosskopf Shawna, author.
Title: Pricing non-marketed goods using distance functions / Dimitris Margaritis (University of Auckland, New Zealand), Rolf Färe (Oregon State University, USA) and Shawna Grosskopf (Oregon State University, USA).
Description: New Jersey : World Scientific, [2018] | Series: World Scientific-Now Publishers series in business ; volume 16 | Includes bibliographical references and index.
Identifiers: LCCN 2018055585 | ISBN 9789813277601 (hc : alk. paper)
Subjects: LCSH: Prices--Mathematical models. | Pricing--Mathematical models.
Classification: LCC HB221 .M338 2018 | DDC 338.5/20151593--dc23
LC record available at https://lccn.loc.gov/2018055585

British Library Cataloguing-in-Publication Data
A catalogue record for this book is available from the British Library.

For any available supplementary material, please visit
https://www.worldscientific.com/worldscibooks/10.1142/11194#t=suppl

Desk Editors: Dr. Sree Meenakshi Sajani/Sylvia Koh

Typeset by Stallion Press
Email: enquiries@stallionpress.com

Printed in Singapore

Preface

Concerns extending from financial systems to ecosystems culminated by the global financial crisis and the poor state of water, air and mineral soil highlight the important role of hard to price real or financial assets for our well-being, present and future. The spectacular financial and ensuing economic and social crises of the last decade spring largely from the mispricing and mismanagement of financial assets, extending from bank capital to complex securities of 'structured finance' used to finance subprime mortgages. Similarly, the roots of environmental degradation largely reflect inefficiencies arising from market and environmental policy failures, the mispricing and mismanagement of emissions to the detriment of our ecosystem.

In this book, we use parametric distance functions as our theoretical and empirical tool to derive shadow pricing rules and their empirical specification and application. One could of course use non-parametric activity analysis or Data Envelopment Analysis (DEA) to implement our pricing rules, which we leave to future efforts.[1] We felt that the pricing side of performance measurement has been somewhat neglected in the efficiency and productivity area. We first thought of producing a monograph on the topic when we worked with Robin Sickles and Chen-Jun Shang after being inspired to try our shadow pricing approach as an alternative to the index number and hedonic approaches presented by Erwin Diewert with respect to housing prices in a measurement workshop organized by Kevin Fox at Coogie Beach about 4 years ago. This effort appears as the first of the four applications in this volume.

[1]We focus on parametric distance functions rather than non-parametric (in the sense of DEA) specification of these distance functions in order to readily exploit the calculus we use to move from primal quantity space to dual price space.

The theoretical (first) half of this volume develops pricing rules for various types of distance functions. Distance functions were introduced to economics by Ronald W. Shephard in 1953. There he defined the input distance function, and in 1970 he extended the model to the output side. He also developed the indirect distance functions which are also included among our functions used to derive shadow prices. We supplement the Shephard-type distance functions with the directional distance function introduced by Luenberger (1992, 1995) and extended by Chambers, Chung and Färe (1998). These are also used to develop pricing rules. Each of the four application chapters employs one of these distance functions.

It has been a long journey with most of the work completed during the regular annual visits of the two US-based authors to the University of Auckland Business School. This book contains the aforementioned application papers co-authored with Robin Sickles, Chen-Jun Shang, Maryam Hasannasab as well as two papers by William Weber. We thank them for their contributions.

Maryam Hasannasab made an enormous contribution reading, critiquing and handling the more technical side of manuscript typesetting for which we are particularly grateful. The manuscript benefited from comments from the participants of the 2016 Workshop on Efficiency and Productivity at the University of Auckland. We also acknowledge Israfil Roshdie's input whose almost endless discussions with Rolf Färe added many insights into our thinking about the book and performance measurement more generally.

Rolf Färe, Shawna Grosskopf and Dimitris Margaritis

About the Editors

Dimitris Margaritis is the Professor of Finance at the University of Auckland Business School. He served as an Advisor, Head of Research and Senior Research Fellow at the Reserve Bank of New Zealand and was a member of the World Bank Project on Financial Reform. He previously taught at the University of British Columbia, University of Washington, Southern Illinois University, SUNY at Buffalo, Waikato Management School and AUT University. His research portfolio covers diverse areas including several contributions to the literature on firm efficiency and productivity, money and banking, corporate finance and asset pricing.

Rolf Färe is the Professor of Economics, and Agricultural and Resource Economics at the Oregon State University. His research is rooted in the areas of production and duality theory, which is documented in 12 books, over 200 refereed journal articles and over 50 contributions to books. He is an ISI most highly cited scholar in the area of economics and finance. He also serves on the editorial board of two journals.

Shawna Grosskopf is the Professor Emerita of Economics at Oregon State University. Her research includes work in performance measurement with applications in environmental productivity, public sector performance, education and health. She serves as the Associate Editor for *Journal of Productivity Analysis* and is on the editorial board of *Health Care Management Science*. She is listed in *Who's Who in Economics* and is an ISI most highly cited scholar in economics and finance.

About the Contributors

William L. Weber is the Professor of Economics at Southeast Missouri State University where he has taught courses in microeconomics, applied economic models, environmental economics and financial institution management for more than 32 years. His research interests are in using duality theory to measure producer performance and to obtain shadow prices of nonmarket goods and services. His applied work has examined banks and other financial institutions, primary and secondary schools, community colleges and universities, agriculture and fisheries, public lands and most recently, knowledge produced by researchers in STEM fields.

Chenjun Shang is a Quantitative Analytic Senior at Freddie Mac, where she develops the house price index model, providing house price forecasts across the US under different scenarios. The forecasts are widely used in the company for mortgage default risk prediction and capital reserve assessment. She does a variant of house price-related analyses, including distressed property evaluation, automated appraisal value assessment and geographic house price risk analysis. She graduated from Rice University with a PhD in Economics. Her field was applied econometrics and productivity and efficiency analysis. Her research works include the stochastic frontier model framework, examination of house price index utilizing Shephard's dual lemma, and study on the productivity change of OECD countries with different methods.

Maryam Hasannasab is a Research Fellow at the University of Auckland Business School. Her research is in optimization, performance measurement and shadow pricing with applications to banking and environmental economics. She has published several papers in the area of Operations Research and Applied Mathematics. She obtained her PhD in Applied Mathematics from Kharazmi University of Tehran in 2018, achieving excellence for her thesis.

Robin C. Sickles is the Reginald Henry Hargrove Chair of Economics and Professor of Statistics at Rice University. He is a member of the Conference on Research in Income and Wealth of the National Bureau of Economic Research. He has written over 90 peer-reviewed articles, 25 book chapters, and has written and edited nine books and special journal issues. He has served as the Editor-in-Chief of the *Journal of Productivity Analysis* and on editorial boards of the *Journal of Applied Econometrics*, *Journal of Business and Economic Statistics*, *Communications in Statistics*, *Empirical Economics*, *Journal of Chinese Economic and Business Studies*, *Southern Economic Journal* and *Journal of Econometrics*.

Contents

Chapter 1

Introduction: Overview of the Book

Rolf Färe, Shawna Grosskopf and Dimitris Margaritis

This book consists of two distinct components. The first sets out the theoretical foundations for using distance functions as tools for shadow pricing, which is especially useful for the case of non-marketed goods, or where prices are missing or do not reflect opportunity costs. Since distance functions represent technology, our shadow prices are based on those underlying technologies. The second half of the monograph consists of four self-standing applications of the tools introduced in part one, and are organized as a sequence of chapters, which are described below. Thus, the reader interested in a specific application can directly proceed to the relevant chapter(s).

The first application is contained in Chapter 8, authored by Färe, Grosskopf, Shang and Sickles, and titled 'Pricing Characteristics: An Application of Shephard's Dual Lemma.' The authors estimate a Shephard input distance function using stochastic frontier methods, among other variations. The estimates are used via Shephard's dual lemma to solve for shadow prices of housing characteristics (e.g., land and structures). In turn these shadow prices are used to construct price indexes, including composite housing price indexes. The authors then compare their results to several variations of indexes based on hedonic methods using the same dataset. They find that the Shephard-based shadow price indexes are less volatile than the hedonic indexes and can avoid problems with multicollinearity.

Chapter 9, 'Shadow Price Estimates of Wetlands in the St. John's Bayou–New Madrid Floodway', written by William L. Weber makes use of a directional output distance function, which accommodates estimation of the (mostly non-priced) environmental benefits of wetlands. The approach exploits the duality between the directional output distance function and the revenue function, to estimate the shadow prices of the public lands surrounding the floodway. He estimates the directional distance function in a parametric (quadratic functional form) linear programming framework. The parameters are used to calculate the shadow prices, which reflect opportunity costs and allow the author to provide estimates of the cost of converting wetlands under a proposal by the Army Corps of Engineers to close a gap in the Mississippi levees.

Chapter 10, 'Pricing Inputs and Outputs in Banking Using Directional Distance Functions', written by Maryam Hasannasab and Dimitris Margaritis applies the pricing rules introduced in part one of the book to estimate the shadow price of bank equity capital and non-performing loans for US banks during the period 2002–2016. The authors estimate a quadratic functional form parameterization of the directional distance function using the Aigner–Chu method. One advantage of this approach compared to standard finance methods based on the capital asset pricing model is that it prices equity for both listed and non-listed banks since it requires no information on the market price of the bank. The authors obtain some interesting results highlighting the risks of overambitious balance sheet expansions during the period prior to the financial crisis. The estimates show excessive levels of shadow prices for equity capital stemming from highly leveraged bank positions conducive to excessive risk-taking behavior. These findings are quite informative since they provide quantitative assessment of the wedge that presumably existed between the shadow price and market price of risk during the period leading up to the subprime crisis, thereby serving as testament to the risk pricing failures underpinning the subprime crisis. Panel regression results confirm the negative relation between core capital and its shadow price. Similarly, the authors find less diversified banks and banks with a larger share of real estate loans in their portfolio face higher equity capital costs.

In the final chapter, William L. Weber employs a network production framework to shadow price knowledge outputs. The title is 'Network Production and Shadow Prices of Knowledge Outputs,' providing a fourth type of application of distance functions to the problem of finding shadow prices.

Thus the four application chapters provide four alternative estimation strategies for estimating shadow prices all based on various distance functions and all exploiting the duality results derived in the theoretical chapters of the book. These can be considered to be complementary to the more familiar hedonic methods to estimate shadow prices.

Chapter 2

Theoretical Underpinnings

Rolf Färe, Shawna Grosskopf and Dimitris Margaritis

The theoretical section of our book consists of seven chapters and an appendix. This chapter introduces the reader to production models upon which the book is based. Together with the appendix, it reviews the basic production theoretical concepts used in modeling the 'black box' technology. This includes the three equivalent input, output and technology sets which transform inputs into outputs, both intended and unintended. Network technologies are introduced in Chapter 6; these consist of connected black box technologies, both static and dynamic.

Distance functions, both Shephard-type as well as directional distance functions, are developed in Chapter 3 and are function representations of the set technologies from this Chapter. They inherit the properties introduced in the appendix and those inherited from their definitions. Shephard-type distance functions are by definition homogeneous, i.e., multiplicative in the scaled vector whereas the directional distance functions satisfy the translation property, which is additive.

Homogeneity and translation are important in particular for choosing functional forms for parameterized versions of these distance functions, as we show in Section 3.4. We conclude that the translog function is appropriate for the Shephard-type distance functions, whereas the quadratic functional form is appropriate for the directional distance functions. These satisfy the inherited properties as well as representing flexible functional forms.

Linking prices to the quantities in our representations of technologies is the basis of our approach to shadow pricing, and relies on duality theory. As an example, consider Shephard's lemma, which states that the gradient vector of a cost function with respect to input prices retrieves the associated input quantities. By distinguishing between primal (quantity) and dual (price) spaces we explain Shephard's Lemma and demonstrate why differentiating distance functions yields (shadow) prices. The mathematics of this relationship is discussed in Chapter 4.

Chapter 6 applies these notions to the shadow pricing of input and output quantities. Beginning with shadow pricing input quantities, we may use either Shephard-type or directional input distance functions. This requires data on those input quantities as well as output quantities. In addition, at least one input price or total cost is also required.

Similarly, output quantities may be shadow-priced by estimating the associated Shephard-type or directional output distance functions. Input and output quantity data is again required along with data on at least one output price or total revenue.

Suppose next that we have input and output quantity data as well as an input price. Can we then estimate a shadow price for outputs? The answer is yes, if we make use of the directional technology distance function and assume profit maximization. These 'cross-over' pricing models are discussed in Section 5.5, and we return to this in Chapter 7.

We turn to shadow pricing with network models of technology in Chapter 6. These models allow for connections among subtechnologies. For example you may have two production processes P^1 and P^2, where some of the outputs from P^1 serve as inputs into P^2. The new challenge is to estimate prices for these intermediate inputs/outputs. Here we employ Shephard-type distance functions. In addition to the usual data requirements, data on intermediate revenue would be required, although we show that introduction of a reallocation constraint can solve this problem.

In Chapter 7, we introduce cost and revenue indirect production models. An example of a cost indirect model is a budget-constrained school district with data on budget, and input prices and the goal of maximizing output given their budget. Here we make use of both directional and Shephard distance functions.

The appendix discusses the axiomatic foundation of our production models as well as the role these play and how they interact.

2.1 Basic Underpinnings

Our pricing models are based on duality theory which requires some basic theoretical building blocks including convex, closed and monotonic sets. And they are developed within the framework of axiomatic production theory where we view production broadly to include, for example, household and firm production. The axioms are found in the appendix to this monograph.

In this chapter, we view the technology as a modified black box in which inputs enter the box and outputs (which may be marketed or non-marketed) exit the box. We open the black box and introduce network technologies in Chapter 6 in order to analyze transfer prices.[1] These technologies may be static or dynamic.

In Section 2.2, we introduce the basic model in which inputs produce intended (marketed) outputs only; in Section 2.3, we generalize the model to include externalities, both desirable and undesirable. These are sometimes referred to as unintended outputs (Murty, Russell and Levkoff, 2012).

2.2 Basic Black Box Technology

We begin with notation: let $x = (x_1, \ldots, x_N) \in \Re_+^N$ be a vector of inputs that are assumed to be non-negative real numbers. Although seemingly harmless, this implies that inputs are divisible; this suggests, for example, that π units of capital could be used in production.[2]

Similarly, we model outputs as a vector $y = (y_1, \ldots, y_M) \in \Re_+^M$, i.e., they too are divisible.

Next, we introduce three equivalent set representations of our technology:

(i) $T = \{(x, y) : x \text{ can produce } y\}$, the technology set
(ii) $P(x) = \{y : (x, y) \in T\}, x \in \Re_+^N$, the output set
(iii) $L(y) = \{x : (x, y) \in T\}, y \in \Re_+^M$, the input set.

Figure 2.1 illustrates these three sets for the simple single-input, single-output case.

[1] They are also useful in modeling technologies with by-products, intermediate goods production, etc.

[2] See Bobzin (1998) for models with indivisible inputs and outputs.

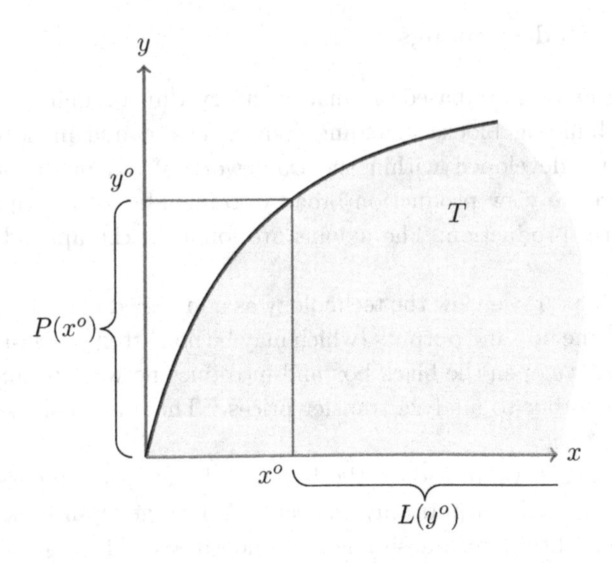

Fig. 2.1: Technology Sets

The area between and including the curved line and the x-axis is the technology set T. It has a boundary and an interior; if the technology is a closed set, then the boundary belongs to the set.

The input set $L(y^o)$ consists of all input vectors along the x-axis including and beyond x^o. The output set $P(x^o)$ is the set of outputs including and below y^o on the y-axis.

If we specify a functional form for a production function, say

$y = \sqrt{x}$,

then the three sets are, respectively,

$$T = \{(x, y) : y \leqq \sqrt{x}, x \in \Re_+, y \in \Re_+\},$$

$$P(x^o) = \{y : y \leqq \sqrt{x^o}, y \in \Re_+\}, x^o \in \Re_+,$$

$$L(y^o) = \{x : (y^o)^2 \leqq x, x \in \Re_+\}, y^o \in \Re_+.$$

Returning to the general case, to prove that these three sets represent the same technology, assume that $(x, y) \in \Re_+^N \times \Re_+^M$ is an arbitrary input–output vector belonging to T, then

$$y \in P(x) \tag{2.1}$$

and

$$x \in L(y), \tag{2.2}$$

by the definitions of the input and output sets. This proves that

$$(x, y) \in T \Longrightarrow y \in P(x) \text{ and } x \in L(y). \tag{2.3}$$

To prove the converse, assume first that $y \in P(x)$. Then $(x, y) \in T$ by the definition of T. Next assume that $x \in L(y)$, then $(x, y) \in T$. Thus we have

$$y \in P(x) \Leftrightarrow (x, y) \in T$$

and

$$x \in L(y) \Leftrightarrow (x, y) \in T.$$

The above yields

Proposition 2.1. $(x, y) \in T \Leftrightarrow x \in L(y) \Leftrightarrow y \in P(x)$. *Hence, the three sets represent the same technology.*

2.3 Production of Unintended Outputs

A firm or farm that produces marketable outputs may also produce unintended outputs as by-products, which could be desirable or undesirable. Examples include the beekeeper producing honey, but also perhaps providing unintended pollination services to the apple grower. Electric utilities produce power but may also emit undesirable by-products such as SO_2 and NOX, which adversely affect human health.

In this section we model production of these types of outputs and by-products. Later we discuss how the individual farms or firms interact with other agents. These interactions are often referred to as the study of externalities.

We start by classifying the two types of unintended outputs as $d = (d_1, \ldots, d_I) \in \Re^I_+$ desirable and $u = (u_1, \ldots, u_J) \in \Re^J_+$ undesirable. This classification is based on the preferences of a consumer, although it could also be done in terms of a producer. We dub a good undesirable if more of that good reduces the utility of the consumer, or equivalently, less of the good increases the utility of the consumer. This is illustrated in Figure 2.2, where we have one undesirable good u and one marketable or intended output y.

Starting at (u, y), more of the intended output y yields higher utility while *less* of the unintended undesirable output u also increases utility.

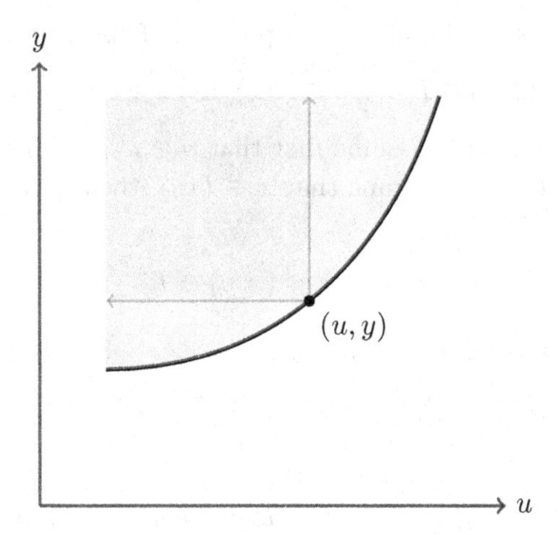

Fig. 2.2: Intended and Undesirable Outputs

Note that the indifference curves in the figure are upward sloping and increasing to the northwest; if we had instead of u included a desirable unintended output d (positive externality) in the figure, the indifference curves would take the standard textbook shape.

Since we consider the unintended outputs (u, d) as unavoidable by-products of production of y, we modify our technology sets to include (u, d), i.e.,

$$T = \{(x, y, u, d) : x \text{ can produce } (y, u, d)\} \tag{2.4}$$

is our expanded technology set. The corresponding output and input sets are

$$P(x) = \{(y, u, d) : (x, y, u, d) \in T\} \tag{2.5}$$

and

$$L(y, u, d) = \{x : (x, y, u, d) \in T\}. \tag{2.6}$$

As before, we have equivalencies among the sets, i.e.,

$$(x, y, u, d) \in T \Leftrightarrow (y, u, d) \in P(x) \Leftrightarrow x \in L(y, u, d). \tag{2.7}$$

We model the 'unavoidability' in production of these by-products with the notion of **Nulljointness**, which we define as

$$(y, u, d) \in P(x), \quad \text{if } d = 0 \Rightarrow y = 0$$

and

$$(y, u, d) \in P(x), \quad \text{if } u = 0 \Rightarrow y = 0.$$

These axioms state if u or d are not produced, then the intended output vector y is zero. With respect to our axioms, see the appendix for more details, we assign them to the extended output vector (y, u, d).

Chapter 3

Distance Functions

Rolf Färe, Shawna Grosskopf and Dimitris Margaritis

In Chapter 2 and the appendix, we focused on set representations of technology and the minimal set of axioms required for us to take advantage of the duality between input and output quantities which constitute our technology sets and their dual prices. Our pricing models make use of calculus, which takes us from quantity to price space; however, calculus is not readily defined for the technology sets we have introduced in Chapter 2. To take advantage of calculus we need a function representation of those technology sets, which is the topic of this chapter. The functions we introduce are distance functions, which are generalizations of the notion of a production function, but without being limited to a single output.

We distinguish between 'multiplicative' and 'additive' distance functions. The multiplicative group consists of Shephard-type distance functions, including the Shephard (1953, 1970) input and output distance functions. The additive distance functions are the directional distance functions including technology, input and output functions. The directional distance functions have their origin in the Allais (1943) surplus function and the Luenberger shortage and benefit functions (Luenberger, 1992, 1995). Here we follow Chambers, Chung and Färe (1998).

In Section 3.1, we define these distance functions, including some of their properties and show how they are related. Specifically, we show how the Shephard distance functions can be derived as special cases of the directional input and output distance functions. In Section 3.2, we turn to parameterization of the distance functions by means of solutions to functional equations, which are assumed to allow for flexible functional forms, sometimes referred to as generalized quadratic.[1] Specifically the resulting functions are linear in their parameters and have a second-order interpretation. We also require that the Shephard distance functions satisfy homogeneity (by their definition) and that the directional distance functions satisfy translation (again by definition). The resulting solutions to the functional equations are our parametric specifications for these functions.

We note that these functional forms are differentiable, implying that we do not need to impose differentiability on the technology.

3.1 Directional Distance Functions

Let $g = (g_x, g_y)$ be a directional vector consisting of an input vector directional $g_x \in \Re_+^N$ and an output directional vector $g_y \in \Re_+^M$. These vectors define the direction in which an input–output vector is projected onto the frontier or boundary of the technology set T. We begin by focusing on the case in which only intended outputs $y \in \Re_+^M$ are produced.

The Directional Technology Distance Function is defined as

$$\vec{D}_T(x, y; g_x, g_y) = \sup\{\beta : (x - \beta g_x, y + \beta g_y) \in T\}, \tag{3.1}$$

i.e., it is the largest feasible value of the projection of (x, y) onto the boundary of T in the direction (g_x, g_y). Figure 3.1 illustrates.

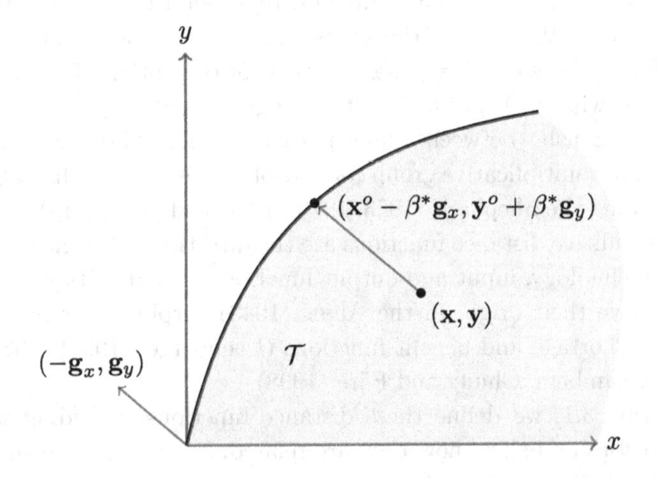

Fig. 3.1: The Directional Technology Distance Function

[1] Other names include second-order approximation, Taylor series approximation.

The input–output vector (x, y) is projected to the frontier of T at

$$(x - \vec{D}_T(x, y; g_x, g_y)g_x, y + \vec{D}_T(x, y; g_x, g_y)g_y).$$

For concreteness we also provide a simple numerical example. We let the technology set be given by

$$T = \{(x, y) : y \leqq 2x, x \geqq 0\}. \tag{3.2}$$

If we choose $(x, y) = (1, 1)$ as well as setting the directional vector $g = (1, 1)$, then

$$\vec{D}_T(1, 1; 1, 1) = \sup\{\beta : (1 - \beta, 1 + \beta) \in T\} \tag{3.3}$$

with the following solution:

$$\begin{aligned}\vec{D}_T(1, 1; 1, 1) = \beta^* &= 1/3,\\ x^* &= 1 - 1/3 = 2/3,\\ y^* &= 1 + 1/3 = 4/3.\end{aligned}$$

The solution depends on the choice of the directional vector, and this choice is typically made by the researcher. One may choose to endogenize the direction vector g; see Färe, Grosskopf and Whittaker (2014) for the optimal choice in non-parametric models and Atkinson and Tsionas (2016) for parametric models.

For now it suffices to note that the directional technology distance function possesses the following characteristics.[2] If inputs and outputs are strongly disposable, i.e., **A.9** holds, then

$$\vec{D}_T.1 \quad \vec{D}_T(x, y; g_x, g_y) \geqq 0 \quad \text{if and only if } (x, y) \in T.$$

Thus under **A.9** (which may be weakened) the directional technology distance function completely characterizes the technology set T. We refer to this property as the **Representation Property**. The implication is that the conditions imposed on T in Chapter 2 and the appendix have analogs in terms of $\vec{D}_T(x, y; g_x, g_y)$.

In addition, from its definition $\vec{D}_T(x, y; g_x, g_y)$ satisfies the **Translation Property**

$$\vec{D}_T.2 \quad \vec{D}_T(x - \alpha g_x, y + \alpha g_y; g_x, g_y) = \vec{D}_T(x, y; g_x, g_y) - \alpha, \quad \alpha \in \Re.$$

[2]See the appendix for additional properties.

This additive condition tells us that translating the data (x, y) along the directional vector translates the value of the distance function by the same factor.

Two other directional distance functions can be derived from $\vec{D}_T(x, y; g_x, g_y)$, namely the **Directional Output Distance Function**

$$\vec{D}_o(x, y; g_y) = \sup\{\beta : (y + \beta g_y) \in P(x)\} \tag{3.4}$$

and the **Directional Input Distance Function**

$$\vec{D}_i(x, y; g_x) = \sup\{\beta : (x - \beta g_x) \in L(y)\}. \tag{3.5}$$

These distance functions are obtained from $\vec{D}_T(x, y; g_x, g_y)$ by setting $g_x = 0$ and $g_y = 0$, respectively, i.e.,

$$\vec{D}_o(x, y; g_y) = \vec{D}_T(x, y; 0, g_y) \tag{3.6}$$

and

$$\vec{D}_i(x, y; g_x) = \vec{D}_T(x, y; g_x, 0). \tag{3.7}$$

Both of these functions satisfy a representation property and a translation property

$$\vec{D}_o.1 \quad \vec{D}_o(x, y; g_y) \geqq 0 \quad \text{if and only if } y \in P(x),$$
$$\vec{D}_o.2 \quad \vec{D}_o(x, y - \alpha g_y; g_y) = \vec{D}_o(x, y; g_y) + \alpha, \quad \alpha \in \Re$$

and

$$\vec{D}_i.1 \quad \vec{D}_i(x, y; g_x) \geqq 0 \quad \text{if and only if } x \in L(y),$$
$$\vec{D}_i.2 \quad \vec{D}_i(x + \alpha g_x, y; g_x) = \vec{D}_i(x, y; g_x) + \alpha, \quad \alpha \in \Re,$$

respectively.

Since

$$(x, y) \in T \Leftrightarrow y \in P(x) \Leftrightarrow x \in L(y), \tag{3.8}$$

it follows that

$$\vec{D}_T.1 \Leftrightarrow \vec{D}_o.1 \Leftrightarrow \vec{D}_i.1. \tag{3.9}$$

Next suppose that unintended outputs (u, d) are also produced. In this case one would like to increase y and d but contract the undesirable output u; thus our augmented directional output distance function would be defined as

$$\vec{D}_o(x, y, u, d; g_y, g_u, g_d) = \sup\{\beta : (y + \beta g_y, u - \beta g_u, d + \beta g_d) \in P(x)\}. \tag{3.10}$$

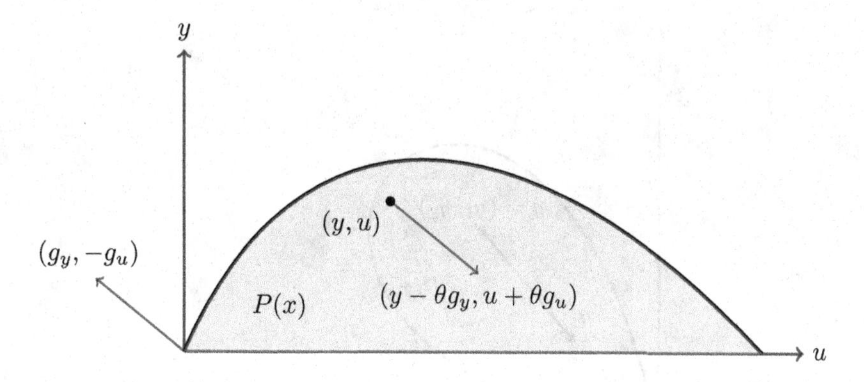

Fig. 3.2: G'-Disposability

For this function to fully represent the technology, i.e.,

$$\vec{D}_o(x, y, u, d; g_y, g_u, g_d) \geqq 0 \Leftrightarrow (y, u, d) \in P(x), \tag{3.11}$$

we need to modify our earlier assumption of **strong disposabilty of outputs**

$$(y, u, d) \in P(x) \text{ and } (y', d') \leqq (y, d), (u' \geqq u) \Rightarrow (y', u', d') \in P(x), \tag{3.12}$$

to allow for **g-disposability of outputs:**

$$(y, u, d) \in P(x), 0 \leqq \theta \leqq 1, \text{ then } (y - \theta g_y, u + \theta g_u, d - \theta g_d) \in P(x).$$

In (y, u) space this takes the form illustrated in Figure 3.2.

Under g-disposability, $\vec{D}_o(x, y, u, d; g_y, g_u, g_d)$ satisfies the representation property. It also satisfies the translation property. We note that the unintended desirable outputs, d, may be treated in the same way we treat the intended outputs, y. Note that if y and d are by themselves strongly disposable, they are by themselves (g_y, g_d)-disposable.

3.2 Shephard's Distance Functions

Shephard (1953, 1970) introduced both an input and an output distance function which represented the input set $L(y)$ and the output set $P(x)$, respectively. He did not, however, define a distance function to represent the technology set T, i.e., there is no Shephard distance function corresponding to the directional technology distance function.[3]

[3]For efforts to introduce a radial distance function representing the technology set, T, see Chambers and Färe (2004).

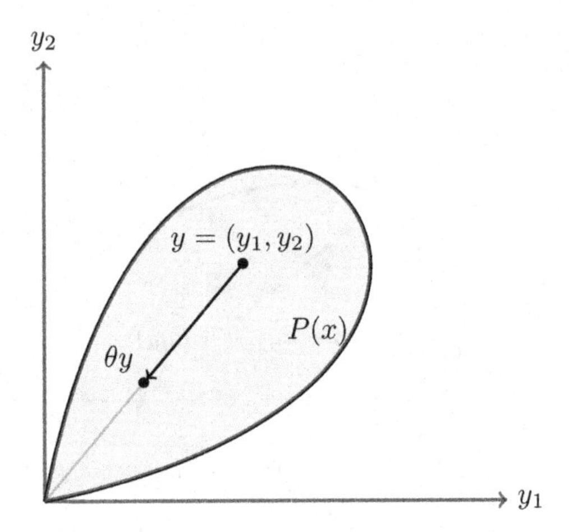

Fig. 3.3: Weak Disposability of Outputs

Shephard's Output Distance Function is defined as

$$D_o(x, y) = \inf\{\theta : y/\theta \in P(x)\}, \tag{3.13}$$

where we are assuming that only intended outputs y are produced. This distance function satisfies the **Representation Property**

$$D_o(x, y) \leqq 1 \Leftrightarrow y \in P(x)\} \tag{3.14}$$

if and only if outputs are **Weakly Disposable** (see Färe and Primont, 1995 for a proof), i.e.,

$$y \in P(x) \text{ and } 0 \leqq \theta \leqq 1 \text{ then } \theta y \in P(x).$$

This condition is illustrated in Figure 3.3.

The output set is given by the 'balloon' emanating from the origin, with output vector $y \in P(x)$. If the output vector is contracted radially toward the origin, i.e., $\theta y, 0 \leqq \theta \leqq 1$, then the contracted output vector is also feasible, i.e., $\theta y \in P(x)$.

The output distance function is homogeneous of degree one in outputs, i.e.,

$$D_o(x, \lambda y) = \lambda D_o(x, y), \lambda \geqq 0. \tag{3.15}$$

Thus, this Shephard distance function has a 'multiplicative' structure, in contrast to the directional distance functions which have an 'additive' structure. Homogeneity of $D_o(x, y)$ follows directly from its definition.

Note that if y is a scalar, then we have

$$D_o(x, \lambda y) = \lambda D_o(x, y) \tag{3.16}$$

and if we take $\lambda = 1/y$ then we have

$$D_o(x, y) = yD_o(x, 1). \tag{3.17}$$

If $D_o(x, y) = 1$, then $y \in IsoqP(x)$, and it is on the boundary of the output set. And then we have

$$y = 1/D_o(x, 1), \tag{3.18}$$

which in this special scalar output case is equivalent to the more familiar production function

$$F(x) = \max\{y : y \in P(x)\} = 1/D_o(x, 1). \tag{3.19}$$

So far we have defined the output distance function in terms of the output set, $P(x)$, but since this set is equivalent to our other set representations of technology, i.e.,

$$(x, y) \in T \Leftrightarrow y \in P(x) \Leftrightarrow x \in L(y), \tag{3.20}$$

we could have defined it in terms of T or $L(y)$.

We define the **Shephard Input Distance Function** in terms of $L(y)$ as

$$D_i(y, x) = \sup\{\lambda : x/\lambda \in L(y)\}, \tag{3.21}$$

again assuming that only intended outputs y are produced. The input distance function also satisfies the **Representation Property**

$$D_i(y, x) \geqq 1 \Leftrightarrow x \in L(y), \tag{3.22}$$

which holds if and only if inputs are **Weakly Disposable**, i.e.,

$$x \in L(y), \theta \geqq 1, \text{then } \theta x \in L(y).$$

If the technology exhibits **Strong Disposability of Inputs**

$$x \in L(y) \text{ and } x' \geqq x \text{ then } x' \in L(y), \tag{3.23}$$

then it also satisfies weak disposability. This follows directly by taking $x' = \theta x$.

Weak disposability allows for backward-bending isoquants and can therefore accommodate congestion which strong disposability excludes. Figure 3.4 is an illustration of this.

In the figure the input vector x is feasible since it is an element of $L(y)$, and its radial (proportional) expansion θx is also capable of producing

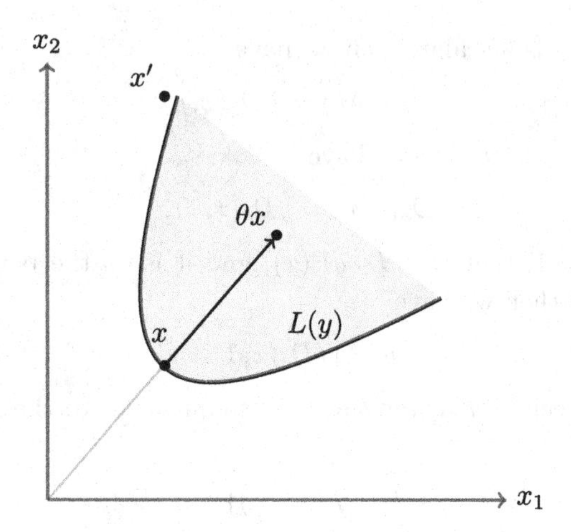

Fig. 3.4: Weak Disposability of Inputs

output vector y, i.e., $\theta x \in L(y), \theta \geqq 1$. Note that x' is not feasible, it lies outside $L(y)$. It represents a vertical expansion of the original input bundle x which would be feasible under strong disposability, illustrating that weak disposability does not imply strong disposability.

The Shephard input distance function — like the output distance function — is homogeneous of degree +1 in its scaled argument, here the input vector x, follows from its definition

$$\begin{aligned} D_i(y, \mu x) &= \sup\{\lambda : \mu x/\lambda \in L(y)\}, \quad \mu > 0 \\ &= \sup\left\{\frac{\lambda}{\mu}\mu : x/\frac{\lambda}{\mu} \in L(y)\right\} \\ &= \mu \sup\left\{\frac{\lambda}{\mu} : x/\frac{\lambda}{\mu} \in L(y)\right\} \\ &= \mu \sup\{\hat{\lambda} : x/\hat{\lambda} \in L(y)\}, \quad \hat{\lambda} = \frac{\lambda}{\mu} \\ &= \mu D_i(y, x). \end{aligned} \tag{3.24}$$

The Shephard distance functions can also model returns to scale. For the case of constant-returns-to-scale (CRS), i.e.,

$$(x, y) \in T, \lambda \geqq 0 \Rightarrow (\lambda x, \lambda y) \in T \tag{3.25}$$

or, $T = \lambda T$ is a cone. This may also be stated in terms of the input and output sets, namely,

$$P(\lambda x) = \lambda P(x), \tag{3.26}$$

or

$$L(\lambda y) = \lambda L(y). \tag{3.27}$$

From these definitions it follows that the two Shephard distance functions satisfy

$$D_o(\lambda x, y) = (1/\lambda) D_o(x, y) \tag{3.28}$$

and

$$D_i(\lambda y, x) = (1/\lambda) D_i(y, x), \tag{3.29}$$

respectively. From these conditions it follows that

$$D_o(x, y) = 1/D_i(y, x) \tag{3.30}$$

if and only if the technology exhibits CRS. To verify this, take

$$D_o(x, y) = 1/D_i(y, x),$$

then

$$\begin{aligned} D_o(\lambda x, y) &= 1/D_i(y, \lambda x) \\ &\qquad \text{(by homogeneity of } D_i(y, x) \text{ in } x) \\ &= 1/(\lambda D_i(y, x)) \quad \text{from above} \\ &= (1/\lambda) D_o(x, y), \end{aligned} \tag{3.31}$$

which shows that $D_o(\lambda x, y) = (1/\lambda) D_o(x, y) \Rightarrow$ CRS. To prove the converse, i.e.,

$$\text{CRS} \Rightarrow D_o(x, y) = 1/D_i(y, x)$$

let

$$\begin{aligned} D_o(x, y) &= \inf\{\lambda : y/\lambda \in P(x)\} \\ &= \inf\{\lambda : x \in L(y/\lambda)\} \\ &= \inf\{\lambda : D_i(y/\lambda, x) \geqq 1\} \\ &= \inf\{\lambda : \lambda D_i(y, x) \geqq 1\} \text{ by CRS} \\ &= \inf\{\lambda : \lambda \geqq 1/D_i(y, x)\} \\ &= 1/D_i(y, x). \end{aligned} \tag{3.32}$$

□

3.3 Shephard vs Directional Distance Functions

Since there is no Shephard distance function which simultaneously scales on inputs and outputs, we only compare his distance functions to the corresponding directional input and output distance functions. Beginning with the directional input distance function, recall its definition

$$\vec{D}_i(x, y; g_x) = \sup\{\beta : (x - \beta g_x) \in L(y)\}, \tag{3.33}$$

where g_x is the directional input vector. If we choose $g_x = x$, i.e., the observed input vector, it follows that:

$$\begin{aligned}\vec{D}_i(x, y; x) &= \sup\{\beta : (x - \beta x) \in L(y)\} \\ &= \sup\{\beta : x(1 - \beta) \in L(y)\} \\ &= \sup\{\beta + 1 - 1 : x(1 - \beta) \in L(y)\} \\ &= 1 - \inf\{(1 - \beta) : x(1 - \beta) \in L(y)\} \\ &= 1 - \inf\{\hat{\beta} : x\hat{\beta} \in L(y)\}, \hat{\beta} = (1 - \beta) \\ &= 1 - 1/D_i(y, x), \end{aligned} \tag{3.34}$$

showing that

$$\vec{D}_i(x, y; x) = 1 - 1/D_i(y, x). \tag{3.35}$$

In the same fashion one can show that the Shephard and directional input distance functions are related by

$$\vec{D}_o(x, y; y) = 1/D_o(x, y) - 1, \tag{3.36}$$

establishing that the Shephard distance functions may be derived as special cases of their directional counterparts.

3.4 Choosing Functional Forms

In this section, we provide a method for finding appropriate functional forms for both Shephard and directional distance functions. We know that by their definitions the Shephard distance functions are homogeneous of degree one in the scaled input or output vector while the directional distance functions satisfy the translation property. Thus, our associated functional forms should be capable of modeling these properties.

In addition, we would like the functional forms to be as 'flexible as possible' while still allowing for these properties. This flexibility is characteristic of the family of generalized quadratic functions[4] which are linear in parameters (convenient for estimation) and have second-order terms.

To set up the functional equation problem we wish to solve, let[5]

$$F : \Re^2 \to F(q_1, q_2) \in \Re \text{ and } h : \Re \to \Re, \rho : \Re \to \Re \tag{3.37}$$

and assume that there exist real constants a_i, a_{ij}, then we say that F is generalized quadratic if it has the form

$$F(q_1, q_2) = \rho^{-1}\left(a_o + \sum_{i=1}^{2} a_i h(q_i) + \sum_{i=1}^{2}\sum_{j=1}^{2} a_{ij} h(q_i) h(q_j)\right). \tag{3.38}$$

Note that if $a_o = 0$ and $a_{ij} = 0$ then the function reduces to a quasi-linear function, Aczél (1966).

Turning to homogeneity, we say that $F(q), q = (q_1, q_2)$ is homogeneous of degree one if

$$F(\lambda q) = \lambda F(q), \quad \lambda > 0 \tag{3.39}$$

and it satisfies instead the translation property if

$$F(q + \alpha q) = F(q) + \alpha, \quad q \in \Re^2, \quad \alpha \in \Re, \tag{3.40}$$

where again homogeneity is by definition a property of Shephard distance functions whereas translation is by definition a property of directional distance functions.

By requiring F to be homogeneous and generalized quadratic we obtain a functional equation. Färe and Sung (1986) showed that this functional equation has two solutions, namely the translog

$$F(q_1, q_2) = a_o + \sum_{i=1}^{2} a_i \ln(q_i) + \sum_{i=1}^{2}\sum_{j=1}^{2} a_{ij} \ln(q_i) \ln(q_j) \tag{3.41}$$

and the mean of order ρ function

$$F(q_1, q_2) = (a_{11} q_1 + a_{22} q_2 + a_{12} q_1^{\rho/2} q_2^{\rho/2})^{1/\rho}, \tag{3.42}$$

[4]This terminology is due to Chambers (1988). They are also referred to as transformed quadratic by Diewert (2002) and second-order Taylor series approximation functions, Färe and Sung (1986).

[5]The following may be generalized to $\Re_+^N$.

where the parameters a_i, a_{ij} are appropriately restricted to satisfy homogeneity. Thus, the Shephard distance functions are appropriately parameterized as translog or mean of order ρ functions.

The functional equation which follows from imposing translation and the generalized quadratic form also has two solutions, see Färe and Lundberg (2006); namely, the quadratic function

$$F(q_1, q_2) = a_o + \sum_{i=1}^{2} a_i q_i + \sum_{i=1}^{2} \sum_{j=1}^{2} a_{ij} q_i q_j \tag{3.43}$$

and

$$F(q_1, q_2) = 1/(2\alpha) \ln \sum_{i=1}^{2} \sum_{j=1}^{2} a_{ij} \exp(\lambda q_i) \exp(\lambda q_j) \tag{3.44}$$

with the appropriate restrictions on the parameters to impose translation. These two are then appropriate choices for the parameterization of the directional distance functions.

Of these four functional forms two of them have no first-order terms, only second-order parameters a_{ij}. Since we are interested in functions that provide the most flexibility with both first- and second-order terms, we conclude that the translog is the appropriate form for the Shephard distance functions and the quadratic form for the directional distance functions.

Chapter 4

Mathematical Underpinnings

Rolf Färe, Shawna Grosskopf and Dimitris Margaritis

One of our goals in this chapter is to provide an intuitive introduction to our method for pricing non-marketed commodities or commodity characteristics. We consider our approach to be a complement to existing methods such as hedonic regressions or contingent valuation. Our main tool is calculus. And the key to finding prices (in price space) for non-marketed goods (which are in quantity space) is the derivative. A derivative is the perfect tool for taking a variable from one linear space — like our quantities — into its dual space, which are the shadow prices we seek.

On this topic Mas-Colell, Whinston and Green (1995, p. 68) write:

> "...just as derivatives of the utility function $u(\cdot)$ with respect to quantities have a price interpretation...the derivatives of the expenditure function $e(\cdot, u)$ with respect to prices have a quantity interpretation..."

Another important and familiar example of this property of derivatives is Shephard's Lemma (1953). This lemma shows that the derivative of the cost function with respect to input prices yields the quantities associated with the input compensated demands. Thus the derivative with respect to a price (an element in price space) is an associated quantity in the dual quantity space.

To understand this and see how we employ the derivatives in finding the shadow prices, we need to define a vector space and its dual. We also introduce linear functions and their interpretation in terms of primal and dual spaces. Finally we show how calculus is related to linear (inner product) functions like the cost function of Shephard's Lemma.

These are the basics we use to understand how distance functions can be applied in pricing non-marketed goods. As an example, when pricing an undesirable output like SO_2 produced as a by-product or unintended output of electricity generation, one may use data on input and output quantities from an electric generating plant, estimate a parametric output distance function and then apply calculus, i.e., Shephard's Dual Lemma, to retrieve its price.

4.1 Linear Functions and their Duals

Here we hope to provide the mathematics required for our pricing rules at a rigorous yet intuitive level. To that end we begin by studying linear functionals defined on $\Re^2$ with their range in $\Re$.[1]

First we note that if $q, q^0, q^1 \in \Re^2$, then

$$q^0 + q^1 \in \Re^2 \tag{4.1}$$

and

$$a \cdot q \in \Re^2, a \in \Re. \tag{4.2}$$

These statements concerning addition and multiplication are defined by components

$$q^0 + q^1 = (q_1^0 + q_1^1, q_2^0 + q_2^1) \in \Re^2 \tag{4.3}$$

and

$$aq = (aq_1, aq_2) \in \Re^2, \tag{4.4}$$

where each component belongs to the real numbers $\Re$.

A functional f defined on a vector space $\Re^2$ is linear if

$$f(q^0 + q^1) = f(q^0) + f(q^1), \;\; q^0, q^1 \in \Re^2 \tag{4.5}$$

and

$$f(aq) = af(q), \;\; q \in \Re^2, a \in \Re. \tag{4.6}$$

The functional $f : \Re^2 \to \Re$ is linear if and only if there exist scalars (p_1, p_2) such that (see, e.g., Fleming, 1977).

$$f(q_1, q_2) = p_1 q_1 + p_2 q_2. \tag{4.7}$$

---

[1]This may be generalized to $\Re^N$.

Familiar examples from economics are value functions such as cost functions, revenue functions and profit functions where $p = (p_1, p_2)$ are given (parametric) prices and $q = (q_1, q_2)$ are the associated variable quantities yielding a value v:

$$v = p_1q_1 + p_2q_2, \tag{4.8}$$

where $p = (p_1, p_2)$ belongs to 'price space' and $q = (q_1, q_2)$ belongs to quantity space, and this function is linear in quantity space. We can also view this from a price space perspective if we take $q = (q_1, q_2)$ as given or parametric and our equation above is a linear function in price space. This points to how a dual space should be defined.

The dual space to $\Re^2$ consists of all continuous functionals defined as

$$\begin{aligned}(f_1 + f_2)q &= f_1(q) + f_2(q),\\ (af)q &= a(f(q)).\end{aligned} \tag{4.9}$$

The space of all of those dual linear functions is denoted as $(\Re^2)^*$. Thus in this dual space, if we let $f_1 = p^1 = (p_1^1, p_2^1)$ and $f_2 = p^2 = (p_1^2, p_2^2), a \in \Re$, (reversing the roles of the p's and q's from above), then

$$\begin{aligned}(f_1 + f_2)q &= (p^1 + p^2)q = p^1q + p^2q,\\ (af)q &= a(f(q)).\end{aligned} \tag{4.10}$$

In the space $\Re^2, (\Re^2)^* = \Re^2$, thus price and quantity spaces coincide mathematically, but as an economist once said, 'one cannot eat prices, only quantities'. Thus, they differ economically.

To show that $(\Re^2)^* = \Re^2$, let $e_1 = (1, 0), e_2 = (0, 1)$ then $q = e_1q + e_2q = (q_1, q_2)$ and

$$\begin{aligned}f(q) &= f(e_1q + e_2q) = f(e_1q) + f(e_2q)\\ &= f(q_1) + f(q_2) = q_1f(e_1) + q_2f(e_2)\\ &= q_1p_1 + q_2p_2,\end{aligned} \tag{4.11}$$

where $p_1 = f(e_1), p_2 = f(e_2)$, thus $\Re^2 = (\Re^2)^*$.[2]

To summarize, if we think of quantity space $\Re^2$ as the primal space, its dual space $(\Re^2)^*$ is the price space, and in our case they are equal: $(\Re^2)^* = \Re^2$.

[2]Continuity follows from the Cauchy–Schwarz inequality, see Fleming (1977).

4.2 Calculus and Dual Spaces

In this section, we show how calculus 'enables you to move' between quantity and price spaces. As in the case of Shephard's Lemma, the derivative of the value function (cost) with respect to input price yields an input quantity, i.e., there is a move from price to quantity space. Eventually, we will use these derivatives to move from distance functions in the quantity space to price space where we retrieve the shadow prices of the non-marketed goods.

A function

$$g : \Re \to \Re,$$

is differentiable (at q) if there exists a linear function $f : \Re \to \Re$ such that

$$\lim_{h \to 0} \frac{g(q+h) - g(q) - f(h)}{h} = 0. \tag{4.12}$$

By homogeneity of f,

$$\lim_{h \to 0} \frac{g(q+h) - g(q)}{h} - f(1) = 0 \tag{4.13}$$

and hence

$$\frac{dg(q)}{dq} = f(1). \tag{4.14}$$

Thus the linear approximation of g and q is

$$f(q) = qf(1) = q\frac{dg(q)}{dq}, \quad \text{where } \frac{dg(q)}{dq} \in \Re^*. \tag{4.15}$$

Hence we have shown for $g : \Re \to \Re$, its derivative is in the dual space of q.

If $g : \Re^2 \to \Re$, then we just redefine g as

$$\hat{g}(q_1) = g(q_1, \overline{q_2}), \tag{4.16}$$

where $\overline{q}_2$ is fixed and the above applies then in each coordinate.

The gradient vector of g is defined as

$$\nabla_q g(q_1, q_2) = \left(\frac{\partial g}{\partial q_1}, \frac{\partial g}{\partial q_2} \right). \tag{4.17}$$

4.3 A Partial Summary

By now we have

(i) introduced a set of axioms that may be applied to our technology
(ii) represented the technology in terms of distance functions, both multiplicative (Shephard) and additive (Directional)
(iii) derived appropriate parametric representations of the two types of distance functions, and finally
(iv) shown how calculus can be used to derive shadow prices.

Chapter 5

Black Box Pricing Models

Rolf Färe, Shawna Grosskopf and Dimitris Margaritis

In this chapter, we derive our pricing models based on the distance functions introduced in Chapter 3. These include both the Shephard 'multiplicative' distance functions and the 'additive' directional distance functions. As we showed in Chapter 3, appropriate functional forms are the translog for the Shephard distance functions and the quadratic for the directional distance functions.

For the Shephard distance functions, we provide two types of shadow pricing models: one model in which quantities adjust to prices, and the second model — its dual case — when prices adjust to quantities. We also consider two alternatives based on data availability: the first when one price is known, and the second when a value is known — either cost, revenue or profit, respectively.

5.1 Shephard's Input Distance Function

The focus in this section is on shadow pricing of input quantities, first when quantities adjust to prices and then when prices adjust to quantities. And we can retrieve the input prices as long as either (i) one price is known or (ii) total cost is known. We assume that input quantities $x = (x_1, \ldots, x_N)$ and output quantities $y = (y_1, \ldots, y_M)$ are known so that we may estimate, using the translog, an input distance function; i.e., $D_i(y, x)$ is also 'known'.

Let input prices be denoted by $w = (w_1, \ldots, w_N)$ and assume that $w \in \Re^N_+$, which also implies that inputs must be strongly disposable. With this data in hand we may describe the cost minimization problem as

$$C(y, w) = \min_x wx \text{ s.t. } D_i(y, x) \geqq 1, \tag{5.1}$$

or in Lagrangian form

$$C(y, w) = \min_x wx - \mu(D_i(y, x) - 1), \tag{5.2}$$

where μ is the Lagrange multiplier. The first-order conditions (FOCs) with respect to inputs x are

$$w - \mu \nabla_x D_i(y, x) = 0. \tag{5.3}$$

Thus, if one input price is known, say w_1, and we are trying to shadow price x_2, then we can use ratios of our FOCs

$$w_2/w_1 = \frac{\partial D_i(y, x)/\partial x_2}{\partial D_i(y, x)/\partial x_1} \tag{5.4}$$

and then we solve for w_2 as

$$w_2 = w_1 \frac{\partial D_i(y, x)/\partial x_2}{\partial D_i(y, x)/\partial x_1}. \tag{5.5}$$

Since the right-hand side consists of known data (x, y, w_1), the shadow price w_2 follows.

Again, suppose that say w_1 is known, then it follows that:

$$c = wx = \sum_{n=1}^{N} w_n x_n$$

is also known, since (5.5) holds for all input prices. This leads us to our next pricing rule.

Suppose that none of the input prices are known, but we instead know total cost, c. Then we can derive the following pricing rule:

$$w = c \frac{\nabla_x D_i(y, x)}{D_i(y, x)}. \tag{5.6}$$

To establish this relation we need to find an expression for the Lagrangian μ; thus consider

$$\begin{aligned}
\tilde{C}(y,w,\alpha) &= \min_x wx - \mu(D_i(y,x) - \alpha) \\
&= \min_x wx - \alpha\mu(D_i(y,x/\alpha) - 1) \\
&= \min w\frac{x}{\alpha}\alpha - \alpha\mu(D_i(y,x/\alpha) - 1) \\
&\quad \text{by homogeneity of the distance function} \\
&= \alpha \min_{\hat{x}} w\hat{x} - \alpha\mu(D_i(y,\hat{x}) - 1), \hat{x} = x/\alpha \\
&= \alpha C(y,w).
\end{aligned} \tag{5.7}$$

Next we take the partial derivative of $\tilde{C}(y,w,\alpha)$ from the first and last lines of (5.7), yielding

$$\partial\tilde{C}(y,w,\alpha)/\partial\alpha = \mu = C(y,w), \tag{5.8}$$

which establishes that the Lagrangian multiplier equals the value of the cost function, i.e.,

$$\mu = C(y,w). \tag{5.9}$$

Together with the FOCs, i.e., using (5.3), we have

$$w = C(y,w) \bigtriangledown_x D_i(y,x). \tag{5.10}$$

Multiplying both sides by x and applying Euler's Theorem yields

$$c = wx = C(y,w)D_i(y,x) \tag{5.11}$$

and

$$C(y,w) = c/D_i(y,x). \tag{5.12}$$

Now our result follows, substituting (5.12) into (5.10), namely,

$$\begin{aligned}
w &= C(y,w) \bigtriangledown_x D_i(y,x), \\
&= c\frac{\bigtriangledown_x D_i(y,x)}{D_i(y,x)},
\end{aligned} \tag{5.13}$$

which provides a pricing rule that only requires data on observed variables.

Alternatively, we can take advantage of the homogeneity of the input distance function and formulate the cost minimization problem as an unconstrained problem (see Färe and Primont, 1995, p. 48), namely

$$C(y,w) = \min_x \frac{wx}{D_i(y,x)}. \tag{5.14}$$

The FOCs associated with this problem are

$$\frac{w}{D_i(y,x)} - \frac{wx}{(D_i(y,x))^2} \nabla_x D_i(y,x) = 0. \tag{5.15}$$

Noting that we have

$$wx = c,$$

and rearranging we have

$$w = c\frac{\nabla_x D_i(y,x)}{D_i(y,x)}, \tag{5.16}$$

which is identical to the pricing rule we derived in (5.6).

5.2 Shephard's Output Distance Function

In this section we derive a formula for estimating shadow prices for outputs based on Shephard's output distance function, $D_o(x, y)$. Empirically this function is estimated using data on inputs $x \in \Re^N_+$ and outputs $y \in \Re^M_+$. Appropriate functional forms are discussed in Chapter 3.

We denote output prices by $p \in \Re^M_+$, which presumes that outputs are strongly disposable, i.e.,

$$y \in P(x), y' \leqq y \Rightarrow y' \in P(x). \tag{5.17}$$

The revenue maximization problem is

$$R(x,p) = \max_y py - \mu(D_o(x,y) - 1), \tag{5.18}$$

where μ is the Lagrangian multiplier.

The FOCs associated with revenue maximization are

$$p - \mu \nabla_y D_o(x,y) = 0. \tag{5.19}$$

Now suppose that p_1 is known and we wish to shadow price output y_2, i.e., to find p_2. By the FOC we have

$$p_2/p_1 = \frac{\partial D_o(x,y)/\partial y_2}{\partial D_o(x,y)/\partial y_1}, \tag{5.20}$$

or

$$p_2 = p_1\frac{\partial D_o(x,y)/\partial y_2}{\partial D_o(x,y)/\partial y_1}. \tag{5.21}$$

Since the right-hand side consists of known data (x, y, p_1), the price of output y_2 can be determined from this expression. When p_1 is known, the pricing rule (5.21) can be used to find the remaining output prices p_m, $m = 2, \ldots, M$, which means that we can also construct total revenue, i.e.,

$$r = py = \sum_{m=1}^{M} p_m y_m.$$

This leads us to our next pricing rule.

Next, suppose that none of the output prices $p_m, m = 1, \ldots, M$ are known, but total revenue r is observed, then we can derive the following pricing expression:

$$p = r \frac{\nabla_y D_o(x, y)}{D_o(x, y)}, \tag{5.22}$$

where the right-hand side consists of observed data (x, y, r).

To continue, we first prove that the Lagrangian multiplier μ equals the revenue function $R(x, p)$. Thus, consider the following set of equalities:

$$\begin{aligned} \tilde{R}(x, p, \alpha) &= \max_y py - \mu(D_o(x, y) - \alpha) \\ &\quad \text{by homogeneity of the distance function} \\ &= \max_y py - \alpha\mu(D_o(x, y/\alpha) - 1) \\ &= \alpha(\max_{y/\alpha} py/\alpha - \mu(D_o(x, y/\alpha) - 1)) \\ &= \alpha R(x, p). \end{aligned} \tag{5.23}$$

Then we obtain

$$\partial \tilde{R}(x, p; \alpha)/\partial \alpha = \mu = R(x, p)s \tag{5.24}$$

and the Lagrangian equals the revenue or value function. Taking this together with the FOCs in (5.19) we obtain

$$p = R(x, p)\, \nabla_y\, D_o(x, y). \tag{5.25}$$

Multiplying both sides with output y and applying Euler's Theorem yields

$$r = py = R(x, p) D_o(x, y), \tag{5.26}$$

or

$$R(x, p) = r / D_o(x, y). \tag{5.27}$$

Substituting this into our pricing expression (5.25) yields the pricing rule for outputs

$$p = \frac{r\, \nabla_y\, D_o(x, y)}{D_o(x, y)}, \tag{5.28}$$

where the right hand side consists of observed data (x, y, r).

Next we take an alternative approach to estimate output shadow prices. Recall that the output distance function $D_o(x,y)$ is homogeneous of degree $+1$ in outputs. This allows us to formulate the revenue maximization problem (5.18) as an unconstrained problem, namely, (see Färe and Primont, 1995, p. 50).

$$R(x,p) = \max_{y} \frac{py}{D_o(x,y)}. \tag{5.29}$$

The FOCs associated with this problem are

$$\frac{p}{D_o(x,y)} - \frac{py}{(D_o(x,y))^2} \nabla_y D_o(x,y) = 0. \tag{5.30}$$

Noting that $py = r$, and rearranging we arrive at the pricing rule in (5.28), namely

$$p = r\frac{\nabla_y D_o(x,y)}{D_o(x,y)}. \tag{5.31}$$

5.3 The Directional Input Distance Function

Next we turn to pricing models using the directional distance functions, beginning with the directional input distance function which is also the function we use presently to estimate shadow prices of non-marketed goods. All of our directional distance functions (input, output and technology) have an additive structure and can be parameterized with a quadratic functional form. The quadratic form allows for zeros in the data in contrast to the translog function (appropriate for our Shephard distance functions) which cannot. Thus if there are zeros in the dataset, the directional rather than Shephard distance functions are preferred.

Assume inputs $x = (x_1, \ldots, x_N)$ and outputs $y = (y_1, \ldots, y_M)$ are known and an input directional vector $g_x = (g_{x_1}, \ldots, g_{x_N})$ is chosen, then the directional input distance function may be parameterized and estimated. To shadow price our input quantities, we first establish the dual relationship to the distance function in price space, namely the cost function. Let $w = (w_1, \ldots, w_N) \in \Re^N_+$ denote input prices, assuming inputs are freely disposable, then the cost minimization problem is

$$C(y,w) = \min_{x} wx \text{ s.t.} \vec{D}_i(x,y;g_x) \geqq 0, \tag{5.32}$$

or written as a Lagrangian problem

$$C(y,w) = \min_{x} wx - \mu\vec{D}_i(x,y;g_x). \tag{5.33}$$

As in previous sections, we seek an interpretation of the multiplier μ; thus consider

$$\begin{aligned}\tilde{C}(y,w,\alpha) &= \min_x wx - \mu(\vec{D}_i(x,y;g_x) - \alpha) \\ &= w\alpha g_x + \min[w(x - \alpha g_x) - \mu(\vec{D}_i(y, x - \alpha g_x; g_x) - 0)] \\ &\quad \text{(by the translation property of the distance function)} \\ &= \alpha w g_x + C(y,w). \end{aligned} \tag{5.34}$$

Differentiating this with respect to α, we find from the first line of (5.34)

$$\partial\tilde{C}(y,w,\alpha)/\partial\alpha = \mu \tag{5.35}$$

and from the last line of (5.34)

$$\partial\tilde{C}(y,w,\alpha)/\partial\alpha = wg_x,$$

thus we have

$$\mu = wg_x, \tag{5.36}$$

which when inserted into our minimization problem yields

$$C(y,w) = \min_x wx - wg_x\vec{D}_i(x,y;g_x) \tag{5.37}$$

as our primal problem. The dual problem is

$$\vec{D}_i(x,y;g_x) = \min_w \frac{wx - C(y,w)}{wg_x}. \tag{5.38}$$

The above two expressions provide the duality between the directional input distance function and the cost function. For the dual expression of the directional input distance function to correspond to its original definition

$$\vec{D}_i(x,y;g_x) = \sup\{\beta : (x - \beta g_x) \in L(y)\}, \tag{5.39}$$

the input requirement sets $L(y)$ must be convex.

Returning to our Lagrangian minimization problem, its FOCs are

$$w - \mu \nabla_x \vec{D}_i(x,y;g_x) = 0, \tag{5.40}$$

thus if w_2 is known and we seek to estimate w_1, then the following may be applied

$$w_1 = w_2\frac{\partial\vec{D}_i(x,y;g_x)/\partial x_1}{\partial\vec{D}_i(x,y;g_x)/\partial x_2}, \tag{5.41}$$

where the right-hand side consists of known data (x, y, w_2) and given the choice of the direction vector g_x. From the above we can derive total cost

$$c = wx = \sum_{n=1}^{N} w_n x_n,$$

which we use as part of the next pricing rule.

If, however, no input price is observed but we do observe total cost, c, then we may derive an alternative pricing condition, namely

$$w = \frac{c \nabla_x \vec{D}_i(x, y; g_x)}{\nabla_x \vec{D}_i(x, y; g_x) x}. \tag{5.42}$$

From the FOCs and $\mu = wg_x$ we find that

$$w = wg_x \nabla_x \vec{D}_i(x, y; g_x). \tag{5.43}$$

Multiplying both sides by x and noting that $c = wx$ we have

$$c = wg_x \nabla_x \vec{D}_i(x, y; g_x) x \tag{5.44}$$

and

$$wg_x = c / \nabla_x \vec{D}_i(x, y; g_x) x. \tag{5.45}$$

Inserting this expression into

$$w = wg_x \nabla_x \vec{D}_i(x, y; g_x) \tag{5.46}$$

results in our second pricing rule

$$w = \frac{c \nabla_x \vec{D}_i(x, y; g_x)}{\nabla_x \vec{D}_i(x, y; g_x) x}, \tag{5.47}$$

where the right-hand side consists of observed data (x, y, c) as well as the chosen direction vector, g_x.

Note that in the denominator we have $\nabla_x \vec{D}_i(x, y; g_x) x$ in contrast to the rule for the radial input distance function with denominator $D_i(y, x)$, since we cannot apply Euler's Theorem. The directional input distance function is not homogeneous in inputs.

As shown in Chapter 3, directional distance functions may be parameterized as a quadratic function, which allows for zeros in the data. The translog does not accommodate zeros in the data, which suggests that the directional distance function is preferred when there are zeros in the data.

5.4 The Directional Output Distance Function

Again we assume that data on inputs $x \in \Re_+^N$ and outputs $y \in \Re_+^M$ are given and a directional output vector $g_y = (g_{y_1}, \ldots, g_{y_M}) \in \Re_+^M$ has been chosen so that the directional output distance function may be estimated. As with the Shephard output distance function, the dual is derived from the revenue maximization problem with output prices $p \in \Re_+^M$

$$R(x,p) = \max_y py \text{ s.t. } \vec{D}_o(x,y;g_y) \geqq 0, \tag{5.48}$$

or in Lagrangian form

$$R(x,p) = \max_y py - \mu \vec{D}_o(x,y;g_y), \tag{5.49}$$

where μ is the Lagrangian multiplier, which as in the cost minimization problem (see 5.34), has the interpretation

$$\mu = pg_y, \tag{5.50}$$

i.e., it is equal to the value of the directional vector.

Inserting this expression into the Lagrangian problem we can derive the primal and dual optimization problems as

$$R(x,p) = \max_y py - pg_y \vec{D}_o(x,y;g_y) \tag{5.51}$$

and

$$\vec{D}_o(x,y;g_y) = \max_p \frac{py - R(x,p)}{pg_y}. \tag{5.52}$$

The revenue function is defined in terms of the directional output distance function in the first problem, and the distance function is retrieved from the revenue function in the second problem. For the retrieved distance function to generate the directional output distance function in Chapter 3, the output set $P(x)$ must be convex.

The FOCs from the Lagrangian problem in (5.49) are

$$p - \mu \nabla_y \vec{D}_o(x,y;g_y) = 0, \tag{5.53}$$

which yields our first pricing rule when one price, say p_2 is known and we seek p_1

$$p_1 = p_2 \frac{\partial \vec{D}_o(x,y;g_y)/\partial y_1}{\partial \vec{D}_o(x,y;g_y)/\partial y_2}. \tag{5.54}$$

The right-hand side consists of observed data (x, y, p_2) and direction vector g_y, allowing us to solve for p_1. Following our earlier argument, (5.54) may then be used to find total revenue

$$r = py = \sum_{m=1}^{M} p_m y_m.$$

In the case when no price $p_m, m = 1, \ldots, M$ is observed, but we instead observe total revenue $r = py$, we can derive our second pricing rule

$$p = \frac{r \nabla_y \vec{D}_o(x, y; g_y)}{\nabla_y \vec{D}_o(x, y; g_y) y}, \tag{5.55}$$

where again the right-hand side consists of observed data, from which the unknown prices may be determined.

The FOCs (5.53) along with $\mu = pg_y$ yield

$$p = pg_y \nabla_y \vec{D}_o(x, y; g_y) \tag{5.56}$$

and by multiplying both sides by y and noting that $r = py$ gives us

$$pg_y = \frac{r}{\nabla_y \vec{D}_o(x, y; g_y) y}, \tag{5.57}$$

hence

$$p = \frac{r \nabla_y \vec{D}_o(x, y; g_y)}{\nabla_y \vec{D}_o(x, y; g_y) y}, \tag{5.58}$$

providing our second pricing rule for outputs using the directional output distance function.

5.5 The Directional Technology Distance Function

Our pricing models up to this point have been based on input or output distance function data (x, y) and in addition we assume that both input and output direction vectors (g_y, g_x) have been chosen, so we can estimate the directional technology distance function $\vec{D}_T(x, y; g_x, g_y)$ using a quadratic functional form.

Recall from Chapter 3 that the directional technology distance function is defined as

$$\vec{D}_T(x, y; g_x, g_y) = \max\{\beta : (x - \beta g_x, y + \beta g_y) \in T\}.$$

Denote input and output prices by $w \in \Re_+^N$ and $p \in \Re_+^M$, respectively, then the profit maximization problem is

$$\pi(w, p) = \max_{x,y} py - wx \text{ s.t. } \vec{D}_T(x, y; g_x, g_y) \geqq 0, \tag{5.59}$$

or as a Lagrangian problem

$$\pi(w,p) = \max_{x,y} py - wx - \mu \vec{D}_T(x,y;g_x,g_y), \tag{5.60}$$

where μ is the Lagrangian multiplier.

Using the translation property of the directional technology distance function

$$\vec{D}_T(x - \alpha g_x, y + \alpha g_y; g_x, g_y) = \vec{D}_T(x,y;g_x,g_y) - \alpha, \tag{5.61}$$

we may show (as in Sections 5.3 and 5.5) that

$$\mu = wg_x + pg_y, \tag{5.62}$$

i.e., μ equals the value of the directional vectors (g_x, g_y).

Inserting this expression into the Lagrangian problem yields both a primal and dual optimization problem

$$\pi(w,p) = \max_{x,y} py - wx - (wg_x + pg_y)\vec{D}_T(x,y;g_x,g_y) \tag{5.63}$$

and

$$\vec{D}_T(x,y;g_x,g_y) = \max_{w,p} \frac{py - wx - \pi(w,p)}{wg_x + pg_y}, \tag{5.64}$$

respectively.

To guarantee that the dual problem yields the directional technology distance function introduced in Chapter 3, the technology T must be convex.

The FOCs associated with the Lagrangian profit maximization problem in (5.60) are

$$p - \mu \nabla_y \vec{D}_T(x,y;g_x,g_y) = 0 \tag{5.65}$$

and

$$-w - \mu \nabla_x \vec{D}_T(x,y;g_x,g_y) = 0. \tag{5.66}$$

The new feature here is that if one output price, say p_1, is known and we seek one input price, say w_1, we can estimate w_1 from

$$w_1 = p_1 \frac{-\partial \vec{D}_T(x,y;g_x,g_y)/\partial x_1}{\partial \vec{D}_T(x,y;g_x,g_y)/\partial y_1}, \tag{5.67}$$

where the right-hand side consists of observed data (x, y), given (g_x, g_y) and p_1.

The expression (5.67) may be used to determine the total (shadow) cost, namely

$$c = wx = \sum_{n=1}^{N} w_n x_n$$

and total (shadow) revenue

$$r = py = \sum_{m=1}^{M} p_m y_m.$$

Of course we may determine p_1 from w_1 and the derivatives of $\vec{D}_T(x, y; g_x, g_y)$, in addition to computing an unobserved output price from an observed output price as in Section 5.5 as well as the same for input prices as in Section 5.3. If no input or output prices are observed, but we do observe profit, then we may compute

$$py = (wg_x + pg_y) \nabla_y \vec{D}_T(x, y; g_x, g_y)y, \tag{5.68}$$

$$wx = -(wg_x + pg_y) \nabla_x \vec{D}_T(x, y; g_x, g_y)x, \tag{5.69}$$

as well as the difference of the above

$$\begin{aligned} \pi = (py - wx) &= (wg_x + pg_y) \\ &\times (\nabla_y \vec{D}_T(x, y; g_x, g_y)y + \nabla_x \vec{D}_T(x, y; g_x, g_y)x). \end{aligned} \tag{5.70}$$

So an output pricing rule based on these is

$$\begin{aligned} p &= \mu \nabla_y \vec{D}_T(x, y; g_x, g_y) \\ &= (wg_x + pg_y) \nabla_y \vec{D}_T(x, y; g_x, g_y) \\ &= \frac{\pi \nabla_y \vec{D}_T(x, y; g_x, g_y)}{\nabla_y \vec{D}_T(x, y; g_x, g_y)y + \nabla_x \vec{D}_T(x, y; g_x, g_y)x} \end{aligned} \tag{5.71}$$

and the input pricing rule becomes

$$w = -\frac{\pi \nabla_x \vec{D}_T(x, y; g_x, g_y)}{\nabla_y \vec{D}_T(x, y; g_x, g_y)y + \nabla_x \vec{D}_T(x, y; g_x, g_y)x}. \tag{5.72}$$

Chapter 6

Network Pricing Models

Rolf Färe, Shawna Grosskopf and Dimitris Margaritis

The black box technology is effectively either a very simple or reduced-form model of production. In this chapter, we build on a growing literature introduced by Färe and Grosskopf and a number of their co-authors and colleagues which attempts to look inside the black box and has come to be known in the DEA world as Network DEA (for an overview, see Färe, Grosskopf and Whittaker, 2014). Here, we use this approach to introduce 'transfer' pricing, which can be framed as a static multi-plant model or as a model over time.

To illustrate our notion of transfer pricing we begin with a simple model which consists of two technologies, P^1 and P^2, which are linked or interact in a system. In this example P^1 uses x^1 inputs which are exogenous to the system to produce two outputs: ${}^1y^f$ units of final output and ${}^1y^i$ units of intermediate outputs which serve as inputs into technology P^2. P^2 uses both intermediate inputs and exogenous inputs x^2 to produce final outputs ${}^2y^f \in \Re^M_+$. This network model is illustrated in Figure 6.1.

These two technologies may be thought of as constituting the inner workings of a static black box technology or as technologies at different time periods. Other examples include a supply chain, intermediate product technology, a school district with multiple campuses, a coal-fired power plant with multiple generators and abatement technologies, and almost any complex organization.

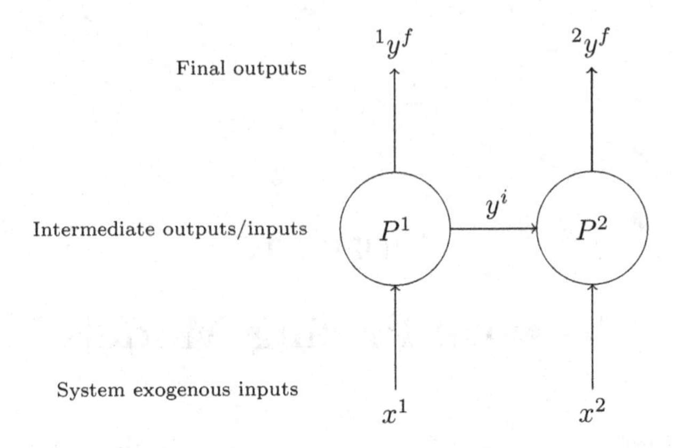

Fig. 6.1: A Network Technology

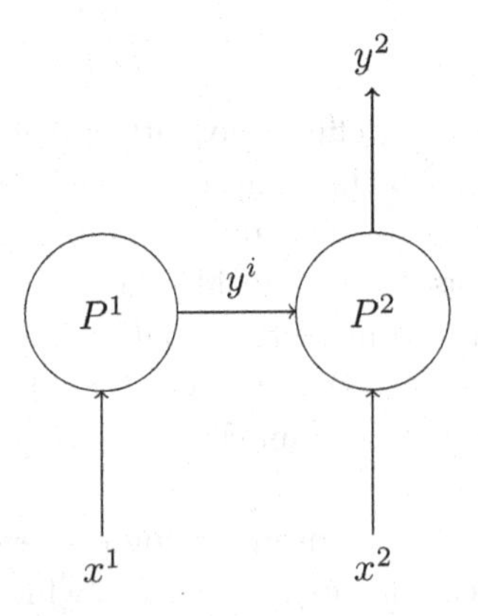

Fig. 6.2: A Reduced Form Network Technology

6.1 A Reduced Form Network Model

In this section, we simplify the model illustrated in Figure 6.1 by restricting the production of technology P^1 to produce only intermediate output/input $y^i \in \Re_+^M$ using inputs x^1 and no final output; technology P^2 produces the final output. See Figure 6.2.

Our objective with this model is to shadow price both the intermediate product vector y^i and final output vector y^2. We model the first technology

$$P^1(x^1) = \{y^i : x^1 \text{ can produce } y^i\}, \tag{6.1}$$

by means of a Shephard output distance function

$$D_o^1(x^1, y^i) = \inf_\lambda\{\lambda : y^i/\lambda \in P^1(x^1)\}. \tag{6.2}$$

The second technology

$$P^2(x^2, y^i) = \{y^2 : (x^2, y^i) \text{ can produce } y^2\}, \tag{6.3}$$

is also modeled as a Shephard output distance function

$$D_o^2(x^2, y^i, y^2) = \inf_\lambda\{\lambda : y^2/\lambda \in P^2(x^2, y^i)\}. \tag{6.4}$$

Recall from expression (3.19) that a single-output production function may be defined as

$$y = F(x) = 1/D_o(x, 1).$$

Thus the two subtechnologies P^1 and P^2, given that y^i and y^2 are scalars, may be modeled as

$$y^i = 1/D_o^1(x^1, 1),$$
$$y^2 = 1/D_o^2(x^2, y^i, 1).$$

Combining these yields

$$y^2 = 1/D_o^2(x^2, 1/D_o^1(x^1, 1), 1),$$

which illustrates how the output y^2 depends on the input x^1, i.e., the technology consists of functions of functions.

In order to derive our pricing models for y^i and y^2, we look to the dual of the output distance function, namely the revenue function to provide our link to price space. The revenue function associated with our network technology is the solution to the following revenue maximization problem:

$$\max_{y^i, y^2} p^i y^i + p^2 y^2,$$
$$\text{s.t.} \quad \begin{aligned} D_o^1(x^1, y^i) &\leqq 1, \\ D_o^2(x^2, y^i, y^2) &\leqq 1, \end{aligned} \tag{6.5}$$

where we are treating the network as a single firm consisting of two subtechnologies. Here, p^i is the unknown price vector of the intermediate output and p^2 is the price vector of y^2, the final product and $p^i, p^2 \in \Re_+^M$. Note that y^i and y^2 are likely to consist of different output vectors[1] with $y^i \in \Re_+^{M^i}$

[1] An exception might be the case where P^2 is a storage technology, in which case we may think of $y^i = y^2$.

and $y^2 \in \Re_+^{M^2}$; here we take

$$y^i, y^2 \in \Re_+^M, \tag{6.6}$$

where $M = M^i + M^2$ and then add sufficiently many zeros to accommodate both types of outputs.

The Lagrangian problem associated with our revenue maximization problem above is

$$\begin{aligned} R(x^1, x^2, p^i, p^2) = \max_{y^i, y^2} & \, p^i y^i + p^2 y^2 \\ & - \mu_1 (D_o^1(x^1, y^i) - 1) \\ & - \mu_2 (D_o^2(x^2, y^i, y^2) - 1). \end{aligned} \tag{6.7}$$

The first-order conditions (FOCs) for this problem are

$$p^i - \mu_1 \nabla_{y^i} D_o^1(x^1, y^i) - \mu_2 \nabla_{y^i} D_o^2(x^2, y^i, y^2) = 0, \tag{6.8}$$

$$p^2 - \mu_2 \nabla_{y^2} D_o^2(x^2, y^i, y^2) = 0. \tag{6.9}$$

From the second set of equalities we have

$$p^2 = \mu_2 \nabla_{y^2} D_o^2(x^2, y^i, y^2). \tag{6.10}$$

Multiply both sides by y^2 and apply Euler's theorem. Since the distance function is homogeneous of degree +1 in y^2, we have

$$r_2 = p^2 y^2 = \mu_2 D_o^2(x^2, y^i, y^2), \tag{6.11}$$

where

$$r_2 = p^2 y^2, \tag{6.12}$$

is the revenue earned from sales of y^2, which for the moment we assume is observed. It now follows that:

$$\mu_2 = \frac{r_2}{D_o^2(x^2, y^i, y^2)}, \tag{6.13}$$

which may be substituted into the appropriate FOC to yield our pricing model for p^2

$$p^2 = \frac{r_2 \nabla_{y^2} D_o^2(x^2, y^i, y^2)}{D_o^2(x^2, y^i, y^2)}. \tag{6.14}$$

The right-hand side is based on the data: r_2, x^2, y^i and y^2, which if available allow us to compute the shadow price p^2.

Next consider the first set of equalities from our FOCs

$$p^i = \mu_1 \nabla_{y^i} D_o^1(x^1, y^i) + \mu_2 \nabla_{y^i} D_o^2(x^2, y^i, y^2). \tag{6.15}$$

Multiply both sides by y^i and apply Euler's theorem to the first distance function, this yields

$$r_i = p^i y^i = \mu_1 D_o^1(x^1, y^i) + \mu_2 \nabla_{y^i} D_o^2(x^2, y^i, y^2) y^i, \tag{6.16}$$

where

$$r_i = p^i y^i \tag{6.17}$$

is the revenue earned from output y^i, which if observed allows us, with some further computation, to arrive at a shadow price for y^i. From our earlier results above we have

$$\mu_2 = \frac{r_2}{D_o^2(x^2, y^i, y^2)} \tag{6.18}$$

and substituting into (6.16) we have

$$r_i = \mu_1 D_o^1(x^1, y^i) + \frac{r_2 \nabla_{y^i} D_o^2(x^2, y^i, y^2) y^i}{D_o^2(x^2, y^i, y^2)}. \tag{6.19}$$

Further manipulation yields

$$\mu_1 = \frac{r_i}{D_o^1(x^1, y^i)} - \frac{r_2 \nabla_{y^i} D_o^2(x^2, y^i, y^2) y^i}{D_o^1(x^1, y^i) D_o^2(x^2, y^i, y^2)}. \tag{6.20}$$

This together with the FOC yields our pricing rule for y^i

$$p^i = \frac{\nabla_{y^i} D_o^1(x^1, y^i)}{D_o^1(x^1, y^i)} \left(r_i - \frac{r_2 \nabla_{y^i} D_o^2(x^2, y^i, y^2) y^i}{D_o^2(x^2, y^i, y^2)} \right) + \frac{r_2 \nabla_{y^i} D_o^2(x^2, y^i, y^2) y^i}{D_o^2(x^2, y^i, y^2)}. \tag{6.21}$$

The right-hand side of this equality requires data on r_i, r_2, x^1, x^2, y^i and y^2. If these are available we can price output vector y^i.

In summary, to price the final output y^2 we need data on r_2, x_2, y^i and y^2, and to price the intermediate output y^i we need additional data namely, r_i and x^1.

Our pricing model above for y^i may be simplified if

$$D_o^2(x^2, \lambda y^i, y^2) = \lambda D_o^2(x^2, y^i, y^2), \lambda > 0, \tag{6.22}$$

i.e., if P^2 is homogeneous of degree one in the intermediate output. In this case we have

$$p^i = \nabla_{y^i} D_o^1(x^1, y^i) \left(r_i - \frac{r_2}{D_o^1(x^1, y^i)} \right) + r_2 \frac{\nabla_{y^i} D_o^2(x^2, y^i, y^2)}{D_o^2(x^2, y^i, y^2)}. \tag{6.23}$$

In the next section, we develop a model in which r_i can be estimated from r_2 as well as the converse. This reduces the burden of data required, especially for r_i. This model is based on the idea that x^1 and x^2 can be freely reallocated between the two subtechnologies, with the restriction that total resources are given, i.e.,

$$x^1 + x^2 \leqq \overline{x}, \tag{6.24}$$

where $\overline{x}$ is the sum of the observed system-wide exogenous inputs.

6.2 Reduced Form with Reallocation of Inputs

Returning to Figure 6.2, we assume in this section that the system exogenous inputs x^1, x^2 can be allocated between the two production units P^1 and P^2. Hence we assume that

$$x^1 + x^2 \leqq \overline{x}, \tag{6.25}$$

where $\overline{x}$ is the total amount of system exogenous inputs, e.g., the observed amount.

We add this reallocation constraint to our revenue maximization problem from Section 6.1, which yields:

$$\begin{aligned} \max_{y^i, y^2, x^1, x^2} \quad & p^i y^i + p^2 y^2 \\ \text{s.t.} \quad & D_o^1(x^1, y^i) \leqq 1,\ D_o^2(x^2, y^i, y^2) \leqq 1 \\ & x^1 + x^2 \leqq \overline{x}. \end{aligned} \tag{6.26}$$

The Lagrangian formulation of this problem is

$$\begin{aligned} R(\overline{x}, p^i, p^2) = \max_{y^i, y^2, x^1, x^2} \ & p^i y^i + p^2 y^2 \\ & - \mu_1 (D_o^1(x^1, y^i) - 1) \\ & - \mu_2 (D_o^2(x^2, y^i, y^2) - 1) \\ & - \mu_3 (x^1 + x^2 - \overline{x}). \end{aligned} \tag{6.27}$$

The FOCs for this problem are

$$\begin{aligned}
p^i - \mu_1 \nabla_{y^i} D_o^1(x^1, y^i) - \mu_2 \nabla_{y^i} D_o^2(x^2, y^i, y^2) &= 0 \\
p^2 - \mu_2 \nabla_{y^2} D_o^2(x^2, y^i, y^2) &= 0 \\
\mu_1 \nabla_{x^1} D_o^1(x^1, y^i) - \mu_3 &= 0 \\
\mu_2 \nabla_{x^2} D_o^2(x^2, y^i, y^2) - \mu_3 &= 0. \qquad (6.28)
\end{aligned}$$

The first two sets of conditions are identical to those we derived in Section 6.1; hence, we can derive our pricing conditions in the same way

$$\begin{aligned}
p^i &= \frac{\nabla_{y^i} D_o^1(x^1, y^i)}{D_o^1(x^1, y^i)} \left(r_i - \frac{r_2 \nabla_{y^i} D_o^2(x^2, y^i, y^2) y^i}{D_o^2(x^2, y^i, y^2)} \right) \\
&\quad + \frac{r_2 \nabla_{y^i} D_o^2(x^2, y^i, y^2)}{D_o^2(x^2, y^i, y^2)} y^i. \qquad (6.29)
\end{aligned}$$

$$p^2 = \frac{r_2 \nabla_{y^2} D_o^2(x^2, y^i, y^2)}{D_o^2(x^2, y^i, y^2)}. \qquad (6.30)$$

The last two FOCs yield

$$\mu_1 \nabla_{x^1} D_o^1(x^1, y^i) = \mu_2 \nabla_{x^2} D_o^2(x^2, y^i, y^2). \qquad (6.31)$$

From Section 6.1 we know that

$$\mu_1 = \frac{r_i}{D_o^1(x^1, y^i)} - \frac{r_2 \nabla_{y^i} D_o^2(x^2, y^i, y^2) y^i}{D_o^1(x^1, y^i) D_o^2(x^2, y^i, y^2)} \qquad (6.32)$$

and

$$\mu_2 = \frac{r_2}{D_o^2(x^2, y^i, y^2)}. \qquad (6.33)$$

Substituting these expressions into (6.31) yields

$$\begin{aligned}
&\nabla_{x^1} D_o^1(x^1, y^i) \left(\frac{r_i}{D_o^1(x^1, y^i)} - \frac{r_2 \nabla_{y^i} D_o^2(x^2, y^i, y^2) y^i}{D_o^1(x^1, y^i) D_o^2(x^2, y^i, y^2)} \right) \\
&\quad = \nabla_{x^2} D_o^2(x^2, y^i, y^2) \left(\frac{r_2}{D_o^2(x^2, y^i, y^2)} \right) \qquad (6.34)
\end{aligned}$$

and we find the following relation between r_i and r_2

$$\begin{aligned}
r_i &= \frac{\nabla_{x^2} D_o^2(x^2, y^i, y^2)}{\nabla_{x^1} D_o^1(x^1, y^i)} \left(\frac{r_2 \nabla_{x^2} D_o^2(x^2, y^i, y^2) D_o^1(x^1, y^i)}{D_o^2(x^2, y^i, y^2) \nabla_{x^1} D_o^1(x^1, y^i)} \right. \\
&\quad \left. + \frac{r_2 \nabla_{y^i} D_o^2(x^2, y^i, y^2) y^i}{D_o^2(x^2, y^i, y^2)} \right). \qquad (6.35)
\end{aligned}$$

Thus, we can solve for r_i if we have data on x^1, x^2, y^i, y^2, r^2. To summarize this section, if we introduce the possibility of reallocation of exogenous system inputs, we can now solve for shadow prices p^i, p^2 as well as compute r_i.

6.3 Reduced Form Model with Individual Firms

In Sections 6.1 and 6.2, we treated our network technology as if it were a single decision-making unit (DMU) and maximized the joint revenue of the two subtechnologies, i.e.,

$$p^i y^i + p^2 y^2, \tag{6.36}$$

under the conditions that the exogenous system inputs x^1, x^2 were given, and then allowed for their reallocation, i.e.,

$$x^1 + x^2 \leqq \overline{x}. \tag{6.37}$$

In this section we treat the two subtechnologies as separate DMUs where the first subtechnology P^1 maximizes its revenue

$$p^i y^i \tag{6.38}$$

and the second technology pursues a goal of minimizing its cost

$$w^i y^i + w^2 x^2. \tag{6.39}$$

A standard example would include a simple supply chain: P^1 produces computer chips which are then purchased by P^2 to make laptops. This general model could also be extended to include externalities. Examples of this type include the beekeeper whose bees pollinate the apple orchard providing a positive externality. Or the upstream paper and pulp firm which emits pollutants which adversely affect the fishing firms downstream. We are modeling an externality whereby the production by P^1 affects the production of P^2 in a way which we assume is outside the market.

We focus here on the case of the positive externality using our black box framework developed in Chapter 5. The main objective is to price the intermediate good y^i, both as an output from P^1 and as an input into P^2. In order to model y^i as an output vector, we follow Chapter 5 and define the output distance function for P^1 as

$$D_o^1(x^1, y^i) = \inf\{\lambda : y^i/\lambda \in P^1(x^1)\}. \tag{6.40}$$

Then by maximizing the revenue for this decision maker, i.e.,

$$R(x^1, p^i) = \max_{y^i} p^i y^i \text{ s.t. } D_o^1(x^1, y^i) \leqq 1. \tag{6.41}$$

As before, we can derive the pricing model

$$p^i = r_i \frac{\nabla_{y^i} D_o^1(x^1, y^i)}{D_o^1(x^1, y^i)}, \tag{6.42}$$

where r_i is the known revenue from selling pollination services and x^1 and y^i are the input and output vectors.

Again, following Chapter 5 we may price y^i as an input into P^2 using an input distance function

$$D_i^2(y^2, x^2, y^i) = \sup\{\lambda : (x^2, y^i)/\lambda \in L^2(y^2)\}, \tag{6.43}$$

where $L^2(y^2)$ is the input requirement set associated with P^2.

By minimizing the cost of both x^2 and y^i

$$\min_{x^2, y^i} w^1 x^1 + w^i y^i \text{ s.t. } D_i^2(y^2, x^2, y^i) \geqq 1, \tag{6.44}$$

we may derive the pricing model from Chapter 5

$$w = (w^2, w^i) = \frac{c \nabla_{(x^2, y^i)} D_i^2(y^2, x^2, y^i)}{D_i^2(y^2, x^2, y^i)}, \tag{6.45}$$

where $c = w^1 x^1 + w^i y^i$ is the known cost for decision maker for P^2. Note that this includes both the cost of exogenous inputs and the intermediate inputs y^i.

When the two DMUs come to an agreement about the production of y^i, we have

$$p^i = w^i, \tag{6.46}$$

implying that

$$r_i \frac{\nabla_{y^i} D_o^1(x^1, y^i)}{D_o^1(x^1, y^i)} = c \frac{\nabla_{(x^2, y^i)} D_i^2(y^2, x^2, y^i)}{D_i^2(y^2, x^2, y^i)}. \tag{6.47}$$

Thus, in order to find a shadow price for y^i we need data on inputs and outputs (x^1, x^2, y^i, y^2) as well as either cost c or revenue r_i. Again, DMU 2 in this case is minimizing cost with respect to both x^2 and y^i.

Chapter 7

Pricing Models Based on Indirect Distance Functions

Rolf Färe, Shawna Grosskopf and Dimitris Margaritis

In this chapter, we introduce pricing models based on cost and revenue indirect distance functions. These functions differ from the distance functions in earlier chapters; their variables are normalized prices and quantities rather than just quantities of inputs and outputs. (see also Färe and Grosskopf, 1994; Shephard, 1974).

These models are appropriate for a variety of enterprises, especially those that are restricted to operating under a budget constraint such as a police department or public school. This type of constraint allows us to model the enterprise as a cost (budget) indirect output correspondence. Similarly, if an enterprise faces a revenue target, one may model it as a revenue indirect input correspondence.

In Section 7.1, we represent the indirect output correspondence by distance functions: both Shephard-type and directional distance functions. As in our earlier chapters, these distance functions form the basis for our indirect pricing models. Similarly, in the subsequent section we introduce distance functions to represent the revenue indirect technology.

7.1 Cost Indirect Distance Functions

Denote the output set by

$$P(x) = \{y : x \text{ can produce } y\}, \quad x \in \Re^N_+,$$

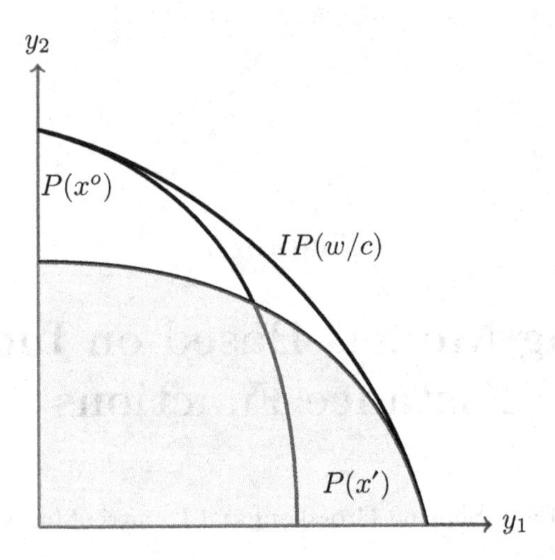

Fig. 7.1: Illustration of $IP(w/c)$

where the input vectors are $x \in \Re_+^N$ and output vectors are $y \in \Re_+^M$. Further assume that input prices are $w \in \Re_+^N$ and that there is a budget $c \in \Re_+$. Then the cost indirect output correspondence is

$$IP(w/c) = \{y : y \in P(x), wx \leqq c\}.$$

In words, this correspondence or output set is the outer envelope of all feasible output sets $P(x)$ that satisfy the budget constraint, i.e., the cost of inputs cannot exceed c.[1] To illustrate $IP(w/c)$, assume that x^o and x' satisfy $wx^o \leqq c$ and $wx' \leqq c$, respectively. These give rise to two direct output sets. These two sets are the part of the indirect model $IP(w/c)$ as shown in Figure 7.1.

We may generalize the indirect model by assuming that we know some of the input prices and their associated subbudget. Thus, let

$$x = (x_s, x_{-s}) \in \Re_+^N$$

be a partition of the input vector, and that we know the prices of the subvector x_s as well as the subbudget associated with that subvector, c_s. We can then define a subvector indirect output distance function as

$$SIP(w_s/c_s, x_{-s}) = \{y : y \in P(x), w_s x_s \leqq c_s, x = (x_s, x_{-s})\}. \tag{7.1}$$

[1]We discuss some of the properties of this set in the appendix.

When $s = N$, we retrieve our original model; however the subvector model is more flexible. For example, it readily models the case in which the enterprise is operating in the short run or has fixed inputs x_{-s} which do not have obvious prices.

Next we return to the original standard cost indirect output model $IP(w/c)$ and define the associated cost indirect (Shephard) output distance function as

$$ID_o(w/c, y) = \inf\{\theta : y/\theta \in P(x), wx \leqq c\}. \tag{7.2}$$

This function satisfies the following two properties: it is homogeneous of degree +1 in outputs, **Homogeneity Property**

$$ID_o(w/c, \lambda y) = \lambda ID_o(w/c, y), \quad \lambda > 0, \tag{7.3}$$

and satisfies the **Representation Property**

$$ID_o(w/c, y) \leqq 1 \Leftrightarrow y \in IP(w/c). \tag{7.4}$$

These are the two properties we need to derive our pricing models.

We denote output prices by p and assume that they belong to $\Re_+^M$. This presumes that outputs are strongly disposable, i.e.,

$$y \in IP(w/c), y' \leqq y \Rightarrow y' \in IP(w/c). \tag{7.5}$$

The cost indirect revenue function is defined by

$$IR(w/c, p) = \max_y\{py : y \in IP(w/c)\}$$

by the representation property

$$= \max_y\{py : ID_o(w/c, y) \leqq 1\}. \tag{7.6}$$

Since $IP(w/c)$ is closed and bounded (compact), the maximum exists; see the appendix. We can specify this problem in Lagrangian form as

$$IR(w/c, p) = \max_y py - \mu(ID_o(w/c, y) - 1), \tag{7.7}$$

where μ is the Lagrangian multiplier. The associated first-order conditions for this problem are

$$p - \mu \nabla_y ID_o(w/c, y) = 0. \tag{7.8}$$

Note that this section follows the structure of Section 5.2, so following that structure we suppose that the price of good one is known and that we seek the price of good two, then by FOCs (7.8) we have

$$p_2/p_1 = \frac{\partial ID_o(w/c, y)/\partial y_2}{\partial ID_o(w/c, y)/\partial y_1}, \tag{7.9}$$

or

$$p_2 = p_1 \frac{\partial ID_o(w/c, y)/\partial y_2}{\partial ID_o(w/c, y)/\partial y_1}. \tag{7.10}$$

Since we have assumed that p_1, w, c and y are known, we can estimate p_2 using the expressions above.

If, however, no price $p_m = 1, \ldots, M$ is known but total revenue $r = py$ is observed, we can derive the following pricing rule to estimate output prices, namely:

$$p = r \frac{\nabla_y ID_o(w/c, y)}{ID_o(w/c, y)}. \tag{7.11}$$

In order to show that this is a valid rule to price outputs without output price data, we proceed by proving that the Lagrangian multiplier in (7.7) equals the value function, i.e.,

$$\mu = IR(w/c, p). \tag{7.12}$$

Let

$$\tilde{IR}(w/c, p, \alpha) = \max_y py - \mu(ID_o(w/c, y) - \alpha)$$

by homogeneity of the distance function

$$= \alpha(\max_y py/\alpha - \mu ID_o(w/c, y/\alpha) - 1)$$

$$= \alpha IR(w/c, p). \tag{7.13}$$

From this we have

$$\frac{\partial \tilde{IR}(w/c, p, \alpha)}{\partial \alpha} = \mu = IR(w/c, p), \tag{7.14}$$

verifying our claim.

We may now rewrite the first-order conditions as

$$p = IR(w/c, p) \nabla_y ID_o(w/c, y). \tag{7.15}$$

Multiplying both sides by y and applying Euler's theorem yields

$$r = py = IR(w/c, p) ID_o(w/c, y) \tag{7.16}$$

and hence our pricing rule from (7.11) above follows

$$p = r \frac{\nabla_y ID_o(w/c, y)}{ID_o(w/c, y)}, \tag{7.17}$$

where the right-hand side consists of observed data w, c, y and r. Since the cost indirect output distance function is homogeneous of degree +1 in outputs, our preferred parameterization of this function is the translog form, see Section 3.4.

Recall that the cost function is defined as

$$\begin{aligned} C(y, w) &= \min_x wx \text{ s.t. } x \in L(y) \\ &= \min_x wx \text{ s.t. } D_i(y, x) \geqq 1, \end{aligned} \tag{7.18}$$

where $L(y)$ is the input requirement set and $D_i(y, x)$ is the input distance function. Given a cost function $C(y, w)$, the cost indirect output correspondence $IP(w/c)$ may be written, for $w > 0$, as

$$IP(w/c) = \{y : C(w, y) \leqq c\} = \{y : C(y, w/c) \leqq 1\}. \tag{7.19}$$

To verify the first equality, let $y^o \in \Re_+^M$ be such that $C(y^o, w) \leqq c$. Since $w > 0$, there exists a vector $x^o \in L(y^o)$, $L(y^o)$ convex, such that $C(y^o, w) = wx^o$. Thus, $y^o \in P(x^o)$ and $wx^o \leqq c$, and hence $y^o \in P(x) = \{y : y \in P(x) \text{ and } wx \leqq c\}$. Conversely, if $y \in P(x)$ and $wx \leqq c$, then $C(y, w) \leqq wx \leqq c$ and it follows that $y \in \{y : C(w, y) \leqq c\}$,
where the second equality follows from homogeneity of degree $+1$ in input prices.

Assume that the technology satisfies Constant Returns to Scale, i.e.,

$$L(\lambda y) = \lambda L(y), \lambda > 0,$$

then the cost function is homogeneous of degree $+1$ in outputs as well:

$$C(\lambda y, w) = \lambda C(y, w), \lambda > 0.$$

Under this condition one can prove that[2]

$$ID_o(w/c, y) = C(y, w/c), \tag{7.20}$$

hence we may substitute the cost function for the distance function in our pricing rules in (7.10) and (7.11). Note that for the pricing rule to hold, a price p_m or revenue $r = py$ must be known.

Using the cost function for estimating shadow prices for output, we have

$$\max_y py - C(y, w), \tag{7.21}$$

which yields

$$p = \nabla_y C(y, w), \tag{7.22}$$

[2]See appendix.

which is the standard marginal cost pricing model which does not require knowledge of any output prices or revenue, but instead requires data c, y, w to estimate $C(y, w)$. This can be compared to the pricing rule in (5.13) in which cost, outputs and inputs are used to find shadow prices for inputs.

To apply the pricing rule

$$p = \nabla_y C(y, w),$$

constant returns to scale is not required, however the maximum over outputs y must exist.

Given the output set $P(x)$, the directional cost indirect output distance function is defined as

$$I\vec{D}_o(w/c, y; g_y) = \sup\{\beta : (y + \beta g_y) \in P(x), wx \leqq c, \} \tag{7.23}$$

and it satisfies the following two conditions:

$$I\vec{D}_o(w/c, y + \alpha g_y; g_y) = I\vec{D}_o(w/c, y; g_y) - \alpha, \ \textbf{Translation} \tag{7.24}$$

and

$$I\vec{D}_o(w/c, y; g_y) \geqq 0 \Leftrightarrow y \in IP(w/c), \ \textbf{Representation.} \tag{7.25}$$

These conditions are used below in our derivation of the pricing rules based on the directional cost indirect output distance function. But first recall that translation plays a role in choosing a functional form for this distance function, namely, the quadratic form is appropriate.

Next introduce the maximization problem

$$I\vec{R}(w/c, p) = \max_y \{py : y \in IP(w/c)\}$$

and by representation:

$$= \max_y \{py : I\vec{D}_o(w/c, y; g_y) \geqq 0\}. \tag{7.26}$$

In Lagrangian form we have

$$I\vec{R}(w/c, p) = \max_y py - \mu I\vec{D}_o(w/c, y; g_y), \tag{7.27}$$

where μ is the Lagrangian multiplier.

The first order conditions for this problem are

$$p = \mu \nabla_y I\vec{D}_o(w/c, y; g_y), \tag{7.28}$$

and if the price of say, good one is known, we can obtain the price of another good say, y_2, from the ratio

$$p_2 = p_1 \frac{\partial \vec{ID}_o(w/c, y; g_y)/\partial y_2}{\partial \vec{ID}_o(w/c, y; g_y)/\partial y_1}. \tag{7.29}$$

Thus, if g_y is given and p_1, w, c and y are known, we can estimate the price of y_2. From above we then can compute the shadow revenue as

$$r = py = \sum_{m=1}^{M} p_m y_m, \tag{7.30}$$

where $p_2, \ldots, p_M$ are derived as above.

Using the translation property and following Section 5.3, we can show that the Lagrangian multiplier is equal to the associated value function, i.e.,

$$\mu = \vec{IR}(w/c, p). \tag{7.31}$$

This condition together with observed cost data c yield the pricing rule

$$p = r \frac{\nabla_y \vec{ID}_o(w/c, y; g_y)}{\vec{ID}_o(w/c, y; g_y)}. \tag{7.32}$$

Thus, if we know r, w, c and y and have a give g_y, we can estimate shadow prices for output vector y.

We return now to our subvector indirect technology

$$SIP(w_s/c_s, x_{-s}) = \{y : y \in P(x), w_s x_s \leqq c_s, x = (x_s, x_{-s})\},$$

where the input vector x is partitioned into the subvectors x_s and x_{-s}. The indirect output distance function defined on this technology is

$$SID_o(w_s/c_s, x_{-s}, y) = \inf\{\theta : y/\theta \in SIP(w_s/c_s, x_{-s})\}, \tag{7.33}$$

and it satisfies homogeneity in y and representation. These properties suffice to derive the following:

$$p_2 = p_1 \frac{\partial SID_o(w_s/c_s, x_{-s}, y)/\partial y_2}{\partial SID_o(w_s/c_s, x_{-s}, y)/\partial y_1} \tag{7.34}$$

and

$$p = r \frac{\nabla_y SID_o(w_s/c_s, x_{-s}, y)}{SID_o(w_s/c_s, x_{-s}, y)}, \tag{7.35}$$

which are the subvector analogs of our standard cost indirect output distance function models. We may also introduce a subvector directional output distance function defined on the output set $SIP(w_s/c_s, x_{-s})$ as

$$S\vec{ID}_o(w_s/c_s, x_{-s}, y) = \sup\{\beta : (y + \beta g_y) \in SIP(w_s/c_s, x_{-s})\}. \quad (7.36)$$

This function satisfies representation and translation, hence we can derive the pricing models

$$p_2 = p_1 \frac{\partial S\vec{ID}_o(w_s/c_s, x_{-s}, y)/\partial y_2}{\partial S\vec{ID}_o(w_s/c_s, x_{-s}, y)/\partial y_1} \quad (7.37)$$

and

$$p = r \frac{\nabla_y S\vec{ID}_o(w_s/c_s, x_{-s}, y)}{S\vec{ID}_o(w_s/c_s, x_{-s}, y)}. \quad (7.38)$$

Since this distance function satisfies the translation property, the quadratic function is our preferred parameterization.

7.2 Revenue Indirect Distance Functions

Recall that technology can be modeled by its input requirement sets/input correspondence

$$L(y) = \{x : x \text{ can produce } y\},$$

where $x \in \Re_+^N$ denotes input and $y \in \Re_+^M$, outputs. In this section we model the revenue indirect technology, i.e., the technology which incorporates revenue targets.

Denote output prices by $p \in \Re_+^M$,[3] which we partition into $(p_s, p_{-s}) = p$. The subvector revenue indirect technology is the defined as

$$SIL(p_s/r_s, y_{-s}) = \{x : x \in L(y), p_s y_s \geqq r_s, y = (y_s, y_{-s})\}. \quad (7.39)$$

The technology models all feasible input vectors $x \in L(y)$ with y_{-s} given, that can generate the revenue r_s, given the prices p_s.

The first two revenue indirect pricing models are based on radial (Shephard) distance functions. Their derivation follows that of Section 5.1; thus we give an abbreviated presentation here.

[3] We assume that outputs are freely disposable, hence non-negative prices are sufficient for duality theory.

The subvector revenue indirect input distance function is defined as

$$\begin{aligned} SID_i(p_s/r_s, y_{-s}, x) &= \sup\{\lambda : x/\lambda \in SIL(p_s/r_s, y_{-s})\} \\ &= \sup\{\lambda : x/\lambda \in L(y), p_s y_s \geq r_s, y = (y_s, y_{-s})\}. \end{aligned} \tag{7.40}$$

This distance function, is homogeneous of degree +1 in inputs x and if we have weak disposability of inputs, it is a complete representation of technology, i.e.,

$$SID_i(p_s/r_s, y_{-s}, x) \geqq 1 \Leftrightarrow x \in SIL(p_s/r_s, y_{-s}). \tag{7.41}$$

Homogeneity and representation are the two properties we need to derive our pricing models, see Section 5.1.

From the cost minimization problem

$$IC(p_s/r_s, y_{-s}, w) = \min wx \text{ s.t. } SID_i(p_s/r_s, y_{-s}, x) \geqq 1, \tag{7.42}$$

or in its Lagrangian formulation

$$IC(p_s/r_s, y_{-s}, w) = \min_x wx - \mu(SID_i(p_s/r_s, y_{-s}, x) - 1), \tag{7.43}$$

again, following Section 5.1, we obtain the two pricing models

$$w_2 = w_1 \frac{\partial SID_i(p_s/r_s, y_{-s}, x)/\partial x_2}{\partial SID_i(p_s/r_s, y_{-s}, x)/\partial x_1} \tag{7.44}$$

and

$$w = c \frac{\nabla_x SID_i(p_s/r_s, y_{-s}, x)}{SID_i(p_s/r_s, y_{-s}, x)}. \tag{7.45}$$

The first model is applicable when one input price is known in addition to observing p_s, r_s, y_s and x. The second model may be applied even if no input prices are known, but cost c must be given. If one input price is known, then the other prices may be retrieved and hence

$$c = \sum_{n=1}^{N} w_n x_n = wx \tag{7.46}$$

may be estimated.

Again, since the distance function is homogeneous in inputs, we favor the translog function as a parametric specification.

Turning to the directional distance function pricing models, we define the subvector revenue indirect directional input distance function as

$$\begin{aligned} S\vec{I}D_i(p_s/r_s, y_{-s}, x; g_x) &= \sup\{\beta : (x - \beta g_x) \in SIL(p_s/r_s, y_{-s})\} \\ &= \sup\{\beta : (x - \beta g_x) \in L(y), \\ &\quad \times p_s y_s \geqq r_s, y = (y_s, y_{-s})\}. \end{aligned} \tag{7.47}$$

This function satisfies both the representation and translation properties. Hence, following Section 5.3, we can derive our two pricing rules

$$w_2 = w_1 \frac{\partial S\vec{I}D_i(p_s/r_s, y_{-s}, x; g_x)/\partial x_2}{\partial S\vec{I}D_i(p_s/r_s, y_{-s}, x; g_x)/\partial x_1} \tag{7.48}$$

and

$$w = c \frac{\nabla_x S\vec{I}D_i(p_s/r_s, y_{-s}, x; g_x)}{S\vec{I}D_i(p_s/r_s, y_{-s}, x; g_x)}. \tag{7.49}$$

Again, since this distance function satisfies translation, we favor the quadratic function as a parametric specification. Finally, note that if one price is known, then we can compute cost,

$$c = \sum_{n=1}^{N} w_n x_n.$$

Chapter 8

Pricing Characteristics: An Application of Shephard's Dual Lemma*

Rolf Färe, Shawna Grosskopf, Robin C. Sickles and Chenjun Shang

8.1 Introduction

During the international financial distresses that led to the Great Recession the balance sheets of banks were (and continue to be) under severe oversight by banking regulators. Basel II requires that bank holding companies have combined Tier 1 and Tier 2 capital ratios of at least 8%. These capital ratios reflect the percentages of a bank's capital to its risk-weighted assets. One of the major assets of a bank is its portfolio of residential mortgages, which typically make up between 20% and 25% of a bank's total assets. As of December 2018 the total residential loans outstanding in the US were roughly US$10.3 trillion, according to the St. Louis Fed (https://fred.stlouisfed.org/series/HHM).

The precipitous drop in the value of such holdings, measured in the valuations from mark-to-market accounting instead of the more conventional book valuations, was a key component in causing the Great Recession.

*We are grateful to W.E. Diewert for his comments and for sharing his data. All remaining errors are ours.

There are a set of reasonable questions to ask about the way in which banks, banking regulators and rating agencies establish the valuation of a bank's real estate holdings and thus the bank's solvency.

(1) What methods do banks use to value their real estate holdings?
(2) Are these methods the same across real estate holdings in different regions of a country?
(3) Are these methods the same across real estate holdings in different countries?
(4) Are these methods transparent and easily calculated?
(5) Are these methods consistent with the economic assumptions underlying the value at risk paradigm used to set reserve benchmarks?

Our paper addresses these questions by providing a transparent and easily implementable methodology for constructing real estate price indexes based on economic assumptions in keeping with the other economic assumptions underlying many of the regulatory criteria used by banking regulators in, for example, the assessment of the value at risk paradigm that provides banks with the rules for setting reserve benchmarks. We use an input distance function to describe the value generating process of residential properties (also referred to as the 'dwelling unit'), which is a euphemism for the output of a production process whose price is the price of the residence. The inputs into the production process are a set of characteristics that a buyer demands, proxied in our empirical analysis by the square footage of the structure, the amount of land on which the structure sits, and the age of the structure.

The specific form of the input distance function is translog, and the shadow prices are derived based on duality theory. We use these shadow prices to construct an imputed residential properties (dwelling unit) price index and compare it to those generated by more conventional hedonic methods. These methods and their advantages and disadvantages have been examined by Good, Sickles and Weiher (2008), among many others.

We implement our modeling approach using a single-output, multi-input distance function. The standard method to estimate the parameters of such an input distance function is to normalize the regression model by moving one of the input variables to the left-hand side and to treat it as the dependent variable and view the unknown distance as a right-hand side error that is combined with the normal idiosyncratic error in the regression model. Of course, this former source of error is bounded due to the bounded nature of the distance function itself.

We utilize several methods to address this aspect of the composed error and compare our imputed residential price index across different approaches. The methods are (1) corrected ordinary least squares with White-type robust standard errors, (2) time dummy least squares regression with White-type robust standard errors (3) stochastic frontier analysis (SFA) (Belotti *et al.*, 2013).

The paper uses data from Diewert (2011) to construct price indexes for residential properties in a small Dutch town using quarterly data from 2005 II to 2008 II. We compare results from our approach, which involves an application of Shephard's Dual Lemma (Shephard, 1953), with methods employed in Diewert and Shimizu (2015) that utilize stratification techniques and various hedonic treatments. Compared with these hedonic regression approaches, our empirical models can simultaneously estimate the shadow prices of the main property characteristics without suffering from typical problems of collinearity among the quality characteristics. The residential property (dwelling unit) price indexes that we derive from our estimations show similar trends to Diewert's results but appear to be less volatile.

8.2 The Theoretical Model

It is known from mathematics that a gradient vector of a function belongs to the dual space of its variables. In economics, a classic example is Shephard's lemma, which says that the derivative of the cost function with respect to a price is an input quantity, i.e., the derivative takes us from the price space to the quantity space. In this paper, we use Shephard's dual lemma (Shephard, 1953), which says that the derivative of the input distance function with respect to an input is an input price. Next, we apply the dual lemma and use it to derive shadow prices of property characteristics.

Assume that a good is endowed with $z = (z_1, \ldots, z_N)$ characteristics. These characteristics in turn generate a value of the good equal to $p \geqq 0$.[1] We model this relation with an input correspondence

$$L(p) = \{z \in \Re_+^N : z \text{ generates value } p\}, \quad p \geqq 0. \tag{8.1}$$

This correspondence can in turn be given a functional representation via Shephard's (1953) input distance function

$$D_i(p, z) = \sup\{\lambda : z/\lambda \in L(p)\}, \tag{8.2}$$

[1]The value of the good is $p = wz$, where $w = (w_1, \ldots, w_N) \in \Re_+^N$ are the unknown prices of the characteristics.

which, with some mild assumptions on $L(p)$ (see Färe and Primont, 1995), provides a complete characterization of the input correspondence, i.e.,

$$D_i(p, z) \geqq 1 \Leftrightarrow z \in L(p). \tag{8.3}$$

Dual to the input distance is the cost function

$$C(p, w) = \min\{wz : z \in L(p)\}, \tag{8.4}$$

where $w \in \Re_+^N$ are the (unknown) prices of the characteristics. From the duality between $C(p, w)$ and $D(p, z)$ we find the shadow price vector of the characteristics to be

$$w = \frac{p \cdot \nabla_z D_i(p, z)}{D_i(p, z)}, \tag{8.5}$$

i.e., the unknown price vector w can be derived from observed data (p, z).

To parameterize the distance function (8.2), we begin by choosing the broad family including the generalized quadratic (Chambers, 1988) and the transformed quadratic (Diewert, 2002) since these functions are linear in their parameters and provide a second-order Taylor approximation. In addition, if these functions are homogeneous of degree +1 in prices (like the input distance function is in inputs), they take two specific functional forms (Färe and Sung, 1986). Either they are quadratic means of order ρ (Denny, 1974; Diewert, 1976) or translog (Christensen, Jorgenson and Lau, 1971). The former function has only second-order parameters, while the translog has both second- and first-order parameters. Having no zeros in our data, we choose to estimate the translog formulation of the distance function (8.2). From these estimates, by applying (8.5), we can derive the desired input-characteristics shadow price vector.

To relate our model to the single-output production models by Thorsnes (1997) and McMillen (2003), assume that the technology $L(p)$ exhibits constant-returns-to-scale (CRS), i.e.,

$$L(\lambda \cdot p) = \lambda \cdot L(p), \quad \lambda > 0. \tag{8.6}$$

Then and only then can the input distance function be written as

$$D_i(p, z) = \frac{1}{p} D_i(1, z), \tag{8.7}$$

noting that p is a scalar. Assuming that z belongs to the isoquant of $L(p)$ so that

$$D_i(p, z) = \frac{1}{p} D_i(1, z) \geq 1, \tag{8.8}$$

then our distance function formulation takes the traditional single-output production function expression,

$$p \leq D_i(1, z). \tag{8.9}$$

Thus the Cobb–Douglas model by McMillen and the CES model of Thorsnes are special cases of (8.9) with a pricing formula (8.5) now given by

$$w = \frac{p \cdot \nabla_z D_i(1, z)}{D_i(1, z)}. \tag{8.10}$$

Upon applying (8.9) we find that

$$w = \nabla_z D_i(1, z). \tag{8.11}$$

8.3 Data, Empirical Model and Price Index Construction of Housing Units

In this section we make use of data kindly provided to us by Professor W. Erwin Diewert and analyzed in Diewert (2011). The data consist of 2289 observations on quarterly sales of detached houses (what we label residential property or dwelling unit) over 14 quarters for town 'A' in the Netherlands. This is a small city (roughly 60,000 inhabitants) and its exact location and of course the name has been masked by Statistics Netherlands. Transactions on dwelling units begin in the first quarter of 2005 and end the second quarter of 2008.

8.3.1 *Empirical model*

8.3.1.1 *General specification*

To justify our choice of the translog model we use in our empirical analyses below, we first note that the input distance function is homogeneous of degree +1 in inputs. It is known, see Färe and Sung (1986), that a homogeneous generalized quadratic function with arguments x_1, x_2 such as

$$\begin{aligned} \varphi^{-1}(F(x_1, x_2)) = a_0 + a_1 f(x_1) + a_2 f(x_2) + b_1 f(x_1) f(x_1) \\ + b_2 f(x_2) f(x_2) + b_3 f(x_1) f(x_2) \end{aligned} \tag{8.12}$$

takes either a translog or generalized mean of order ρ functional form. As the latter function has only second-order parameters, the translog is the preferred choice in our empirical analysis. In the application below we specify the arguments as characteristics of property services, which we have denoted as $z_i, i = 1, \ldots, n$.

In the case of detached residential properties, we treat each dwelling unit as the output whose price is influenced by a number of characteristics. The main variables used are:

p: value of the residential dwelling unit;
L: land area of the property;
S: floor space area of the structure;
A: age of the structure.

The land area L, floor space area S and structure age A are treated as the three input characteristics ($z_i, i = 1, 2, 3$), and p is the value of output. The translog input distance function is specified as

$$\begin{aligned}\ln D_i &= \alpha_0 + \alpha_1 \ln p + \frac{1}{2}\alpha_{11}(\ln p)^2 + \beta_1 \ln S + \beta_2 \ln L + \beta_3 \ln A \\ &\quad + \frac{1}{2}\beta_{11}(\ln S)^2 + \frac{1}{2}\beta_{22}(\ln L)^2 + \frac{1}{2}\beta_{33}(\ln A)^2 + \beta_{12} \ln S \ln L \\ &\quad + \beta_{13} \ln S \ln A + \beta_{23} \ln L \ln A + \gamma_1 \ln S \ln p + \gamma_2 \ln L \ln p \\ &\quad + \gamma_3 \ln A \ln p. \end{aligned} \tag{8.13}$$

The assumptions of homogeneity of degree +1 in inputs and symmetry imply the following restrictions on the parameters:

$$\beta_1 + \beta_2 + \beta_3 = 1, \tag{8.14}$$

$$\sum_{l=1}^{3} \beta_{kl} = 0, \quad k = 1, 2, 3, \tag{8.15}$$

$$\gamma_1 + \gamma_2 + \gamma_3 = 0, \tag{8.16}$$

$$\beta_{kl} = \beta_{lk}, \quad k, l = 1, 2, 3. \tag{8.17}$$

Utilizing these restrictions, the distance function can be rewritten as

$$\begin{aligned}\ln D_i &= \alpha_0 + \alpha_1 \ln p + \frac{1}{2}\alpha_{11}(\ln p)^2 + \beta_1 \ln \frac{S}{A} + \beta_2 \ln \frac{L}{A} + \ln A \\ &\quad + \frac{1}{2}\beta_{11}\left(\ln \frac{S}{A}\right)^2 + \frac{1}{2}\beta_{22}\left(\ln \frac{L}{A}\right)^2 + \beta_{12} \ln \left(\frac{S}{A}\right) \ln \left(\frac{L}{A}\right) \\ &\quad + \gamma_1 \ln \frac{S}{A} \ln p + \gamma_2 \ln \frac{L}{A} \ln p. \end{aligned} \tag{8.18}$$

From the model, we know that the shadow price vector is

$$w^s = \frac{p \cdot \nabla_z D_i(p, z)}{D_i(p, z)}, \tag{8.19}$$

where p is the value of output and z is the vector of all inputs. Denoting w_S, w_L and w_A as the shadow prices of the structure, the land, and the age of the structure, respectively, we can then derive the explicit expressions for the shadow prices of the input characteristics as

$$w_S = \frac{p}{S}(\beta_1 + \beta_{11} \ln S + \beta_{12} \ln L + \beta_{13} \ln A + \gamma_1 \ln p), \tag{8.20}$$

$$w_L = \frac{p}{L}(\beta_2 + \beta_{22} \ln L + \beta_{12} \ln S + \beta_{23} \ln A + \gamma_2 \ln p), \tag{8.21}$$

$$w_A = \frac{p}{A}(\beta_3 + \beta_{33} \ln A + \beta_{13} \ln S + \beta_{23} \ln L + \gamma_3 \ln p). \tag{8.22}$$

8.3.1.2 *Specification with constant-returns-to-scale assumption*

To make our setting comparable to the traditional hedonic regression model, we consider the assumption of CRS. As shown in Section 8.2, we can derive the relation between the output price and the input distance function under CRS assumption as in equation 8.9. The inequality is captured by the distance to the frontier by $D_i(1, z)$. Substituting the translog functional form into (8.9), we can obtain the following regression equation:

$$\begin{aligned} \ln p = \alpha_0 + \beta_1 \ln S + \beta_2 \ln L + \beta_3 \ln A + \frac{1}{2}\beta_{11}(\ln S)^2 + \frac{1}{2}\beta_{22}(\ln L)^2 \\ + \frac{1}{2}\beta_{33}(\ln A)^2 + \beta_{12} \ln S \ln L + \beta_{13} \ln S \ln A + \beta_{23} \ln L \ln A + \ln D_i. \end{aligned} \tag{8.23}$$

We can see that it is the same as the general specification when one sets $\alpha_{11} = \gamma_1 = \gamma_2 = 0$. This model with CRS assumption is, in essence, the same as the hedonic regression with S, L and A as the characteristics.

Again, we impose the assumption of homogeneity of degree 1. Compared with the general case there are now no terms on the right-hand side involving $\ln p$, and thus we no longer need to estimate the γ coefficients nor do we need to address the right-hand side endogeneity of terms interacting with the endogenous $\ln p$ terms. The homogeneity condition now implies equations (8.14), (8.15) and (8.17). With these three constraints, we can rewrite equation (8.23) as

$$\begin{aligned} \tilde{\ln p} = \alpha_0 + \beta_1 \ln \frac{S}{A} + \beta_2 \ln \frac{L}{A} + \frac{1}{2}\beta_{11}\left(\ln \frac{S}{A}\right)^2 \\ + \frac{1}{2}\beta_{22}\left(\ln \frac{L}{A}\right)^2 + \beta_{12} \ln \frac{S}{A} \ln \frac{L}{A}, \end{aligned} \tag{8.24}$$

where $\tilde{\ln p} = \ln p - \ln A$. Under this new specification the shadow prices of the three characteristics are

$$w_S = \frac{1}{S}(\beta_1 + \beta_{11} \ln S + \beta_{12} \ln L + \beta_{13} \ln A), \tag{8.25}$$

$$w_L = \frac{1}{L}(\beta_2 + \beta_{22} \ln L + \beta_{12} \ln S + \beta_{23} \ln A), \tag{8.26}$$

$$w_A = \frac{1}{A}(\beta_3 + \beta_{33} \ln A + \beta_{13} \ln S + \beta_{23} \ln L). \tag{8.27}$$

8.3.2 *Construction of the price index*

For comparison purposes, we use the matched model Fisher index discussed in Diewert (2011). Diewert constructs price indexes for land and for structures that make up the dwelling unit of a particular age, and we do likewise. Dwelling units are grouped into 45 cells consisting of three categories for land area (small, medium, large), three categories for structures (small, medium, large) and five groups for age. The break points for the size of land and structure are chosen in a way that about 50% of the units fall in the medium group and roughly 25% units are in the small and large group, respectively. The break points for land area are $L_1 = 160\,\mathrm{m}^2$ and $L_2 = 300\,\mathrm{m}^2$, and the break points for structure size are $S_1 = 110\,\mathrm{m}^2$ and $S_2 = 140\,\mathrm{m}^2$. Age of the structure is identified by when the structure was built and ranges from 1960 to 2008. For houses built in 2000–2008, $A = 2$; $A = 3$ for 1990–1999 and so on.[2] Using the structure (or land) prices derived from the above model, we define w_n^t to be the average structure (land) price for properties in cell n that were sold in period t,

$$w_n^t = \frac{\sum_{i \in n} w_i^t z_i^t}{\sum_{i \in n} z_i^t} = \frac{\sum_{i \in n} w_i^t z_i^t}{z_n^t}, \tag{8.28}$$

where z_i^t and w_i^t represent the structure (land) area and its corresponding shadow price in cell n. As there is no transaction in some cells across two compared periods, we define $S(s,t)$ to be the set of cells n that have at least one transaction in each of the quarters s and t. The indexes are then computed over these matched components. The Laspeyres (L) and Paasche

[2]In Diewert (2011), the range of age A is 0–4. To accommodate our use of the translog distance function, we shift the range of A from 2 to 6.

(P) indexes for periods s and t are

$$w^L(s,t) = \frac{\sum_{n \in S(s,t)} w_n^t z_n^s}{\sum_{n \in S(s,t)} w_n^s z_n^s}, \quad (8.29)$$

$$w^P(s,t) = \frac{\sum_{n \in S(s,t)} w_n^t z_n^t}{\sum_{n \in S(s,t)} w_n^s z_n^t}. \quad (8.30)$$

Diewert constructs the (ideal) Fisher index by taking the geometric mean of the above two indexes

$$W^F(s,t) = [w^L(s,t) w^P(s,t)]^{\frac{1}{2}}. \quad (8.31)$$

Two sets of indexes are constructed for both structure and land prices. One is a fixed Fisher index, which uses the first quarter as the base period. The other is a chained index: we construct the Fisher index for every two consecutive periods, and the chained index for period t is computed as:

$$I_F^t = W^F(1,2) W^F(2,3) \cdots W^F(t-1,t).$$

8.4 Regression and Results

8.4.1 *General specification*

We utilize three different regression methods to estimate the input distance function (8.13). The methods are (1) corrected ordinary least squares with White-type robust standard errors,(2) time dummy least squares regression with White-type robust standard errors and (3) stochastic frontier analysis (SFA) (Belotti *et al.*, 2013). The results are shown in Table 8.1. The input distance function has long been utilized in theoretical papers to measure

Table 8.1: Regression Results — General Specification

	COLS			Time Dummy			SFA		
Parameter	Coefficient	Std.Err.	t	Coefficient	Std.Err.	t	Coefficient	Std.Err.	z
cons	−0.6104	0.3629	−1.68	−1.0422	0.3457	−3.01	−0.6055	0.2792	−2.17
$(\ln \hat{p})^2$	−0.2730	0.0430	−6.35	−0.1998	0.0412	−4.85	−0.2730	0.0355	−7.68
$\ln(S/A)$	−0.1221	0.2733	−0.45	0.1830	0.2595	0.71	−0.1224	0.2062	−0.59
$\ln(L/A)$	−0.8229	0.2140	−3.84	−0.8394	0.2050	−4.09	−0.8227	0.1722	−4.78
$\ln A$	0.0237	0.0505	0.47	0.0178	0.0478	0.37	0.0238	0.0474	0.50
$(\ln(S/A))^2$	−0.0203	0.0237	−0.86	0.0124	0.0236	0.53	−0.0203	0.0197	−1.03
$(\ln(L/A))^2$	−0.0943	0.0304	−3.10	−0.0952	0.0289	−3.29	−0.0942	0.0252	−3.74
$\ln(S/A)\ln(L/A)$	−0.0434	0.0494	−0.88	0.0251	0.0474	0.53	−0.0435	0.0373	−1.17
$\ln(S/A)\ln \hat{p}$	0.0912	0.0881	1.04	−0.0684	0.0837	−0.82	0.0913	0.0677	1.35
$\ln(L/A)\ln \hat{p}$	0.3451	0.0777	4.44	0.3023	0.0744	4.07	0.3450	0.0666	5.18

the technical efficiency level of a production process. The input distance is bounded from below by unity, which represents a technically efficient level of production. The use of the distance function in empirical work can be traced back to Färe, Grosskopf and Lovell (1985) wherein linear programming was used to estimate non-parametric distance functions and measure technical efficiency. Starting in the 1990s, researchers also considered parametric functions and used econometric methods for estimation. Lovell *et al.* (1994) specified a translog distance function and used OLS to estimate the parameters. The translog functional form was also used in Coelli and Perelman (1996, 2000) and also was estimated using OLS.

In our application, the land, structure and vintage (age) of a detached property are regarded as the inputs, which are used to 'produce' this property, and input distance D_i gives us an estimate of the (in)efficiency level compared to the efficient frontier. As discussed in previous sections, we choose the translog functional form to model the input distance function. In most empirical studies using translog input distance functions with m outputs and k inputs, the negative of the logged kth input or the negative of the logged mth output is treated as the dependent variable and is regressed upon the remaining terms, and the negative of the logged input distance is treated as an error term. As the property's value is endogenously determined by its characteristics, we put $-\ln p$ on the left-hand side and rearrange the distance function as below

$$\begin{aligned}-\ln p = {} & \frac{\alpha_0}{\alpha_1} + \frac{1}{2}\frac{\alpha_{11}}{\alpha_1}(\ln p)^2 + \frac{\beta_1}{\alpha_1}\ln\frac{S}{A} + \frac{\beta_2}{\alpha_1}\ln\frac{L}{A} + \frac{1}{\alpha_1}\ln A \\ & + \frac{1}{2}\frac{\beta_{11}}{\alpha_1}\left(\ln\frac{S}{A}\right)^2 + \frac{1}{2}\frac{\beta_{22}}{\alpha_1}\left(\ln\frac{L}{A}\right)^2 + \frac{\beta_{12}}{\alpha_1}\ln\left(\frac{S}{A}\right)\ln\left(\frac{L}{A}\right) \\ & + \frac{\gamma_1}{\alpha_1}\ln\frac{S}{A}\ln p + \frac{\gamma_2}{\alpha_1}\ln\frac{L}{A}\ln p - \frac{1}{\alpha_1}\ln D_i. \end{aligned} \tag{8.32}$$

Note that by the definition of the input distance function, $D_i \geq 1$, thus $-\ln D_i \leq 0$ and can be interpreted as a one-sided error. Now the objective function (8.32) fits into the production frontier model paradigm, and we can utilize frontier methods for estimation, such as those developed in Stata (Belotti *et al.*, 2013).

OLS can be used to estimate the coefficients of the distance function. After obtaining the estimates of all coefficients, we correct the estimated intercept by adding the largest positive residual such that the adjusted function bounds all the observed points from below. This gives us the corrected OLS (COLS) estimates. Though our observations are detached properties with access to basically the same amenities, we still use robust errors in the regression to account for possible heteroskedasticity.

Before we utilize the COLS method for estimation, note that there exist cross-products of $\ln p$ and other characteristics and squared $\ln p$ on the right-hand side. Thus we consider a two-stage regression and instrument $\ln p$ in the first stage, selecting regressors from the set of characteristics as well as their higher-order terms and cross-product terms to predict $\ln p$. The selection of regressors is empirically based; our goal is to predict $\ln p$ as accurately as possible with the data on hand. The regression we use for predicting $\ln p$ is

$$\ln p = \beta_0 + \beta_1 \ln L + \beta_2(\ln L)^2 + \beta_3(\ln A)^2 + \beta_4 \ln R + \beta_5(\ln S)(\ln L) + \beta_6(\ln L)(\ln A) + \beta_7 Shed + \beta_8 Iso + \beta_9 Main, \quad (8.33)$$

where R is the number of rooms in the house, $Shed$ is the number of sheds, Iso is the degree of isolation of the house, and $Main$ represents the degree of maintenance outside the structure. The adjusted R^2 of this regression is 0.8432, and the correlation between the predicted $\ln \hat{p}$ and $\ln p$ is 0.9185. We substitute the predicted $\ln \hat{p}$ for $\ln p$ on the right-hand side of (8.32) and then conduct the second-stage regression. As stated in the beginning of this section, we consider three regression methods for the second stage. The R^2 using COLS is 0.8438, and estimated coefficients are shown in Table 8.1.

The data begin in the first quarter of 2005 and end in the second quarter of 2008. Considering that property prices might be affected by the date of the transaction due to changing market conditions and other factors proxied by time, we add dummy variables to account for yearly and quarterly effects and reestimate the model by COLS. The R^2 improves to 0.8689.

As noted in Coelli and Perelman (1996), both the linear programming technique (see, for example, Färe *et al.*, 1993) and the COLS method assume the distance to the fully efficient frontier is due entirely to technical inefficiency. To account for the effect of data noise, we can employ stochastic frontier methods. Adding a pure noise term to equation (8.32), we now have a composite error $\epsilon_i = v_i - lnD_i = v_i - u_i$, where u_i is the idiosyncratic error assumed to be $i.i.d.N(0, \sigma_v)$; u_i is our logged input distance, representing technical inefficiency. Here we assume u_i follows the half-normal distribution, i.e., $u_i = |z_i|$, $z_i \sim N(0, \sigma_u)$, and use standard ML techniques for these estimates. These and other stochastic frontier models can be estimated using Stata (Belotti *et al.*, 2013). The stochastic frontier estimates from equation (8.32) are also reported in Table 8.1. The R^2 for this model (using the maximum likelihood estimates to construct the explained variation relative to the total variation in the dependent variable) is 0.8436.

8.4.2 *A further comparison with the methods of Diewert and Shimizu (2015)*

Diewert and Shimizu (2015) employed hedonic regression techniques to decompose the price of residential property in Tokyo into land and structure components, and constructed constant quality indexes for land and structure prices, respectively. In this section we use three different models from Diewert and Shimizu (2015) to fit our real estate data from town 'A' in the Netherlands. We also construct the price indexes for structures and land and compared these results with those derived above.

In traditional hedonic regression models, the price of one unit of commodity under study is assumed to depend on a function of its characteristics. Diewert (2003), among others, provides the microeconomic support for this method. If one assumes that an agent can consume a hedonic commodity Z with a set of characteristics $z = (z_1, \ldots, z_k)$ and other commodity X, then the consumption of Z units of the hedonic commodity gives a subutility of $f(z_1, \ldots, z_k)$, and the consumption of Z and X together generates utility $u = U(Z, X)$. Denote p^t and w^t to be the prices of the general commodity and hedonic commodity at period t, respectively. The consumer then faces a standard cost minimization problem

$$\min_{X,Z}\{p^t X + w^t Z : U(X, Z) = u^t\}.$$

Under some regulatory conditions, the price of the hedonic commodity can be expressed as

$$w^t = \rho_t f(z_1, \ldots, z_t).$$

That is, the price of the hedonic good is the product of some time-dependent effects and the utility a consumer gets from its characteristics. The hedonic regression methods are widely used in real estate studies. These methods model property value based on actual choices of people, and they can be modified to take into account the interaction between the characteristics of the property itself and the effects of the surrounding environment. Some limitations also exist with the classic hedonic pricing model as they do in our approach that utilizes the input distance function. For example, the hedonic model assumes that the price of the residential dwelling unit can change immediately after the change in one or some of its characteristics, whereas in reality, there may be a substantial time lag. The hedonic model also assumes that there are a variety of properties in the market so that consumers can choose the one with the desired combination of characteristics, which is only possible if the market is deep. Another problem is multicollinearity among characteristics, which we comment on further in our analysis below. Finally, consumer may find that some properties have all the good characteristics, while some alternatives are inferior in all aspects.

The basic paradigm in Diewert and Shimizu (2015) is referred to as a builder's model, which is based on the assumption that the value of a residential property is the sum of the value of the land on which it is built and the construction cost of its structure. Considering that the structure's price usually falls as the structure ages, they assume the constant quality structure to be a function of its age and a constant depreciation rate over all time periods. Following the notation used above, we can specify the model as,

$$p_{it} = w_{L,t}L_{it} + w_{S,t}(1 - \delta A_{it})S_{it} + \epsilon_{it}, \quad i = 1, \ldots, N(t); \; t = 1, \ldots, 14, \tag{8.34}$$

where $N(t)$ is the number of properties sold in period t. One concern about this model is the multicollinearity between the land size and structure size: we would expect a larger house structure to be built with a larger land area. Our data show that the correlation between land size and structure size is 0.6278. Thus the coefficient estimates of land and structure may not be reliable in the sense that small variations in the data may result in erratic changes in the estimates. To deal with this multicollinearity, Diewert and Shimizu (2015) assumed the price of a constant quality structure was proportional to a property construction cost index published by the relevant authority. This method was also employed in Diewert (2011) as one approach to exploring the price change of residential properties, in which the index used was the New Dwelling Output Price Index (NDOPI) published by the Central Bureau of Statistics of Netherlands. The resulting land price index from Diewert (2011) will be included as part of our comparison. Rather than directly using the results from Diewert (2011), we consider three applicable methods from Diewert and Shimizu (2015) for two reasons: (1) there exist slight differences between the data used here and the data analyzed in Diewert (2011) — summary statistics are reported in Table 8.2; (2) the focus of Diewert (2011) was on the price index construction of the residential properties rather than their characteristics,

Table 8.2: Summary Statistics Comparison

	Diewert	Ours
Number of observations	2289	2280
Average sale price	190.13	189.76
Average land area	257.6	258.98
Average structure area	127.2	127.09

while Diewert and Shimizu (2015) focused more on the decomposition of property prices into land and structure components.

We set the constant quality structure price to be proportional to the NDOPI mentioned above, the same index used in Diewert (2011), as we examine the same dataset. As Diewert assumes that the price of the structure is proportional to the construction cost index, we follow this assumption in order to provide results as comparable as possible to the hedonic methods he uses and set $w_{S,t} = w_S P_{C,t}$, where P_{C_t} represents the exogenous cost index. The model can then be written as

$$p_{it} = w_{L,t} L_{it} + w_S P_{C_t}(1 - \delta A_{it}) S_{it} + \epsilon_{it},$$
$$i = 1, \ldots, N(t); \;\; t = 1, \ldots, 14. \tag{8.35}$$

We denote this model as DS0, corresponding to the basic builder's model in Diewert and Shimizu (2015).[3] Coefficients of this nonlinear model are estimated by minimizing the mean squared error of the residual term and $w_{L,t}$ is interpreted as a suitable constant quality land price for all residential properties sold in period t. The constant quality land price index for quarter t is defined by Diewert and Shimizu to be

$$I_{L,1t} = w_{L,t}/w_{L,1}. \tag{8.36}$$

The age-adjusted constant quality structure is defined to be $(1 - \delta A_{it}) S_{it}$ and the corresponding structure price index for quarter t is defined by Diewert and Shimizu to be

$$I_{S,1t} = (w_S P_{C_t})/(w_S P_{C_1}) = P_{C_t}/P_{C_1}. \tag{8.37}$$

[3]In Diewert and Shimizu (2015), the basic builder's model also included the 21 dummy variables indicating different wards in Tokyo, to account for possible differences in land prices. In our dataset, all observations are detached residential properties with access to basically the same amenities; thus the difference in locations has little effect on property prices. The R^2 is quite satisfactory in our regression.

The second model employs splines on both the land size and structure age. Empirical evidence indicates that the growth rate of the property land prices vary with land size. To model the possible changes in land prices as land area increases, Diewert and Shimizu (2015) divided all observations into three groups based on the land size and assumed that the land price in each group was linear in land size. Diewert (2011), which analyzed the same dataset as we do, also considered the possibility of changing land prices over different land area ranges in one of his approaches to measure the property price. The method used in Diewert (2011) was the same as Diewert and Shimizu (2015) wherein all observations were grouped into three categories based on their land sizes and land price was assumed to be piecewise linear in land areas. To make our results comparable to those from Diewert (2011), we divided our data into the same three groups, with break points at $L_1 = 160$ and $L_2 = 300$. This generates a grouping with approximately 50% of the properties in the middle group and 25% in the lower and upper groups. The piecewise linear relative land value function is thus specified as

$$f_L(L_{it}) = \mathrm{DL}_{it,1}\gamma_1 L_{it} + \mathrm{DL}_{it,2}(\gamma_1 L_1 + \gamma_2(L_{it} - L_1)) + \mathrm{DL}_{it,3}(\gamma_1 L_1 + \gamma_2(L_2 - L_1) + \gamma_3(L_{it} - L_2)), \quad (8.38)$$

where $\mathrm{DL}_{it,j}$, $j = 1, 2, 3$ are the land dummy variables with $\mathrm{DL}_{it,j} = 1$ indicating that the property falls into category j and $\mathrm{DL}_{it,j} = 0$ meaning that observation i is not in category j. The unknown parameters to be estimated are the γ_k, $k = 1, 2, 3$.

We also group all the observations into three categories based on the age of the structure in order to be consistent with Diewert as he points out that depreciation rates will not be the same for structures of different ages. The break points are chosen to be $A_1 = 1$ and $A_2 = 2$, and the categorical dummy variables for ages are denoted as $\mathrm{DA}_{it,j}$, $j = 1, 2, 3$, with $\mathrm{DA}_{it,j} = 1$ indicating that the property is in category j. This is intended to ensure that the three groups have roughly the same size. However, due to the categorical nature of the data and the unequal number of properties in each of the five age categories (ages are indicative of the building decade and range from 0 to 4, with structures with ages new to 10 years having a much larger number than the other 4 categories) the actual number of properties in the three groups are unequal and set at 1052, 481 and 474, respectively. The piecewise linear depreciation function of the structure's age is defined as

$$g_A(A_{it}) = 1 - (\mathrm{DA}_{it,1}\delta_1 A_{it} + \mathrm{DA}_{it,2}(\delta_2 A_1 + \delta_2(A_{it} - A_1)) + \mathrm{DA}_{it,3}(\delta_1 A_1 + \delta_2(A_2 - A_1)) + \delta_3(A_{it} - A_2)), \quad (8.39)$$

where δ_k, $k = 1, 2, 3$ are the unknown parameters modeling the depreciation schedule of different structure ages.

Now the new model with generalizations to accommodate land size and structure age can be defined as

$$p_{it} = w_{L,t} f_L(L_{it}) + w_S P_{C_t} g_A(A_{it}) S_{it} + \epsilon_{it}. \quad (8.40)$$

We denote this model as DS1. This is also a nonlinear regression model, and we can see that the three land relative value parameters (γ's) and the 14 land time parameters ($w_{L,t}$'s) cannot all be identified unless we impose some normalization condition. Thus, we use the normalization that $\gamma_1 = 1$. Note that in this extended model, the marginal land prices for each category, the γ's, are assumed to be the same over all time periods, while $w_{L,t}$ represents the time change in land price for properties in all groups. Thus the constant quality land price index is again defined as in (8.36) for period t, and the constant quality structure price index is again defined as in (8.37).

In addition to these main characteristics such as the land and structure size, the price of a residential property is also affected by other factors concerning the design of the structure and use of the land space. The model can be further extended to adjust for number of rooms, which affect the quality of the structures. To model the effects of the number of rooms, we utilize the same technique that first divides all observations into three groups and then define a piecewise linear function of the number of rooms. In our data, the number of rooms, denoted as N_{it}, ranges from 2 to 10. We first transform the variable to be $R_{it} = N_{it} - 2$, which ranges from 0 to 8, and then divide the properties into three groups based on R_{it}. The break points for R_{it} are chosen to be $R_1 = 2$ and $R_2 = 3$. Let $\mathrm{DR}_{it,j}$ be the dummy variable for the number of rooms, and the piecewise linear function of R_{it} is defined as

$$g_B(R_{it}) = \theta_1 + \mathrm{DR}_{it,1} R_{tn} + \mathrm{DR}_{it,2}(\theta_2 R_1 + \theta_3(R_{it} - R_1)) + \mathrm{DR}_{it,3}(\theta_2 R_1 + \theta_3(R_2 - R_1) + \theta_4(R_{it} - R_2)). \quad (8.41)$$

Then model incorporating this adjustment of structure quality is specified as

$$p_{it} = w_{L,t} f_L(L_{it}) + w_S P_{C_t} g_A(A_{it}) g_B(R_{it}) S_{it} + \epsilon_{it}, \quad (8.42)$$

Table 8.3: Land Price Indexes Comparison

Period	DS0	DS1	DS2	COLS	TD	SFA	Diewert
1	1.0000	1.0000	1.0000	1.0000	1.0000	1.0000	1.0000
2	1.1709	1.1480	1.1282	1.0259	1.0263	1.0259	1.1386
3	1.1620	1.1628	1.1454	1.0185	1.0191	1.0185	1.1653
4	1.0187	1.0286	1.0299	0.9971	0.9975	0.9971	1.0421
5	1.1436	1.1359	1.1337	1.0143	1.0147	1.0143	1.1189
6	1.1890	1.1644	1.1447	1.0508	1.0507	1.0508	1.1818
7	1.2767	1.2596	1.2313	1.0601	1.0602	1.0601	1.2350
8	1.1734	1.1642	1.1385	1.0446	1.0445	1.0446	1.1326
9	1.2417	1.2192	1.1848	1.0969	1.0967	1.0969	1.2120
10	1.1478	1.1548	1.1340	1.0768	1.0770	1.0768	1.1955
11	1.2436	1.2373	1.2075	1.0756	1.0759	1.0756	1.1775
12	1.1375	1.1403	1.1242	1.0835	1.0833	1.0835	1.1159
13	1.0160	1.0083	1.0025	1.0776	1.0774	1.0776	1.0507
14	1.1674	1.1550	1.1361	1.0914	1.0916	1.0914	1.0965

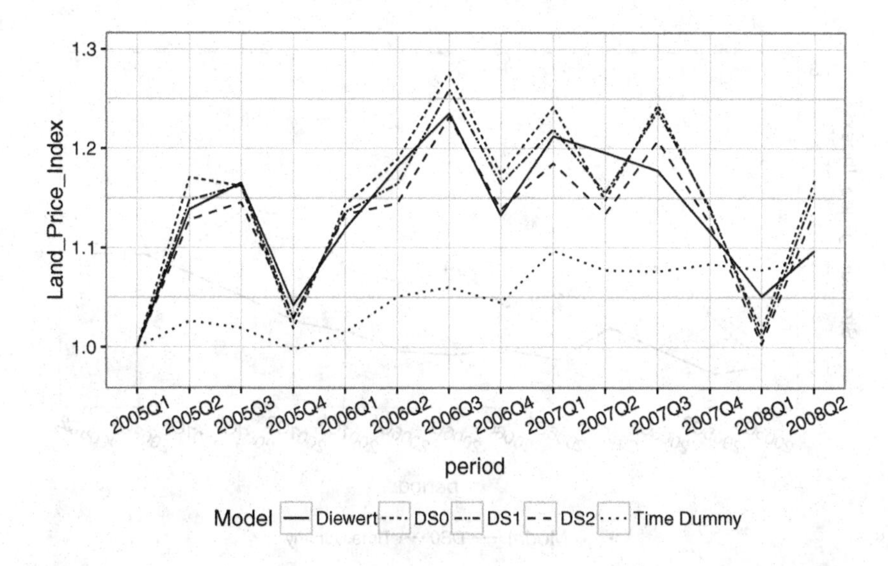

Fig. 8.1: Land Price Index Comparison

where of course w_S does not vary with time in order to address the high collinearity between structure and land sizes. As the case in DS1, not all parameters can be identified unless some normalizations are made. We thus add two normalization conditions that $\gamma_1 = 1$ and $\theta_1 = 1$, and denote this model as DS2. The constant quality price indexes for land and structure are defined the same as in the previous two models.

Table 8.4: Structure Price Index Comparison

Period	DS0	COLS	TD	SFA
1	1.0000	1.0000	1.0000	1.0000
2	0.9929	1.0470	1.0466	1.0470
3	1.0152	1.1095	1.1075	1.1095
4	1.0395	1.0648	1.0636	1.0648
5	1.0071	1.0747	1.0734	1.0747
6	1.0172	1.0612	1.0603	1.0612
7	1.0122	1.1023	1.1004	1.1023
8	1.0152	1.0865	1.0846	1.0865
9	1.0344	1.0985	1.0972	1.0985
10	1.0445	1.1505	1.1482	1.1505
11	1.0688	1.1632	1.1602	1.1632
12	1.0921	1.1263	1.1243	1.1263
13	1.1134	1.1126	1.1114	1.1126
14	1.1134	1.1268	1.1251	1.1268

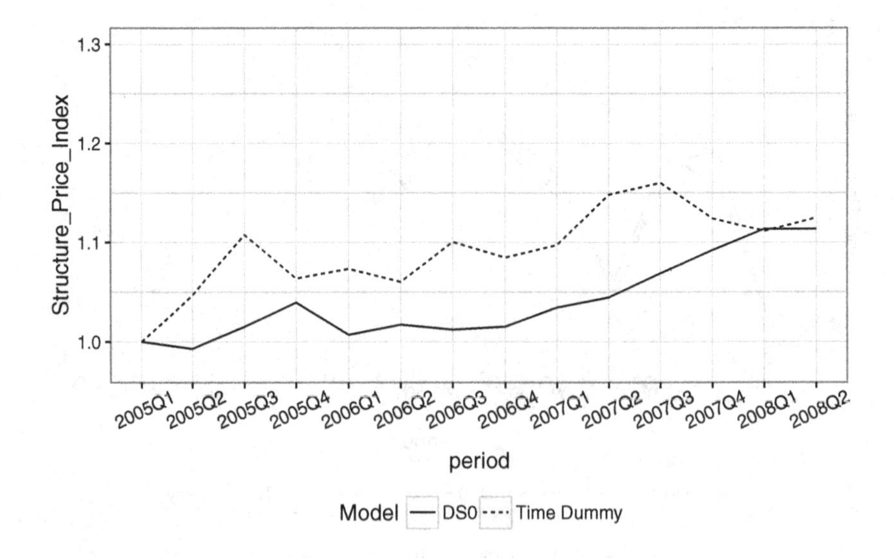

Fig. 8.2: Structure Price Index Comparison

The land price indexes constructed from different models are shown in Table 8.3 and plotted in Figure 8.1. The three indexes derived using our model are almost identical, and not affected by different regression methods. Thus we only plot one set of indexes from our model (the one with time dummies) and compare its pattern with those from hedonic regression methods. The indexes derived from the

Table 8.5: House Price Index and NDOPI

Time period	Num. of obs.	NDOPI	Fisher fixed-base house price index	Fisher chained house price index
1	157	1.0000	1.0000	1.0000
2	155	0.9929	1.0240	1.0240
3	154	1.0152	1.0682	1.0784
4	155	1.0395	1.0490	1.0408
5	163	1.0071	1.0444	1.0408
6	175	1.0172	1.0668	1.0575
7	157	1.0122	1.0731	1.0734
8	152	1.0152	1.0768	1.0671
9	159	1.0344	1.0683	1.0895
10	194	1.0445	1.1189	1.1148
11	137	1.0688	1.1220	1.1247
12	187	1.0921	1.1132	1.1048
13	148	1.1134	1.1107	1.1045
14	187	1.1134	1.1058	1.1119

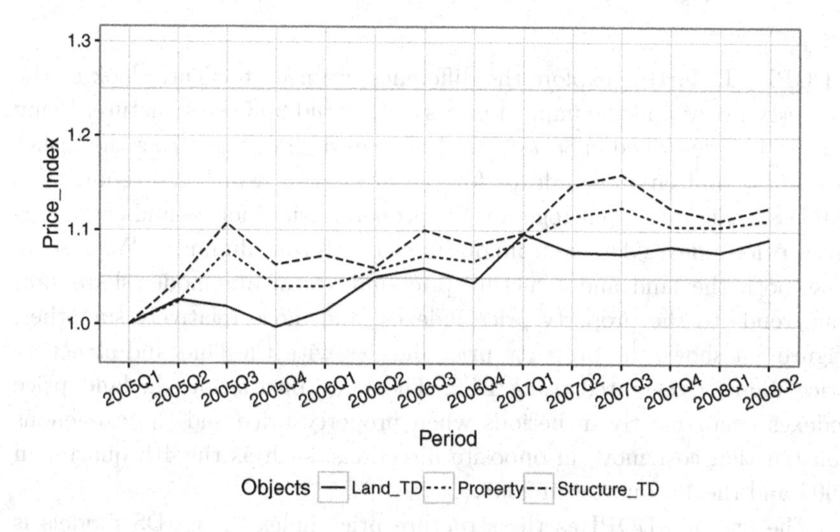

Fig. 8.3: Price Decomposition using Distance Function

DS models show much larger fluctuations compared to our results. The structure price indexes are shown in Table 8.4 and plotted in Figure 8.2. The three indexes from our model again almost coincide with each other as with the land price indexes, and we only plot the set of indexes with time dummies. We can see our endogenously generated indexes exhibit different trends than the exogenous construction cost index

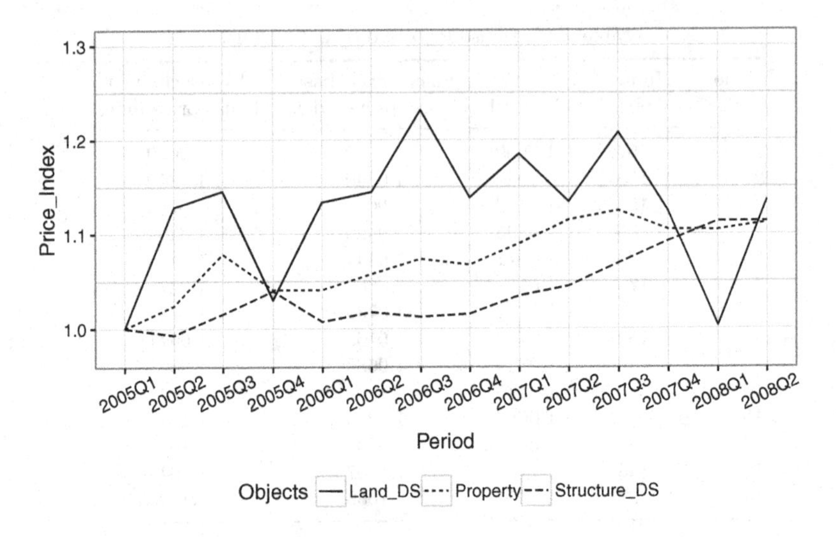

Fig. 8.4: Price Decomposition using Hedonic Regression

NDOPI.[4] To further explore the difference, we need to jointly look at the property prices and the implied prices of the land and the structure. Using the method described in Section 8.4.1, we can similarly construct the Fisher fixed-base and chained indexes for the properties, which are reported in Table 8.5. Figure 8.3 put together the property price indexes and characteristics price indexes derived from our model with time dummies. We observe that both the land and structure price indexes of our model share similar trends to the property price indexes, and move relatively smoother. Figure 8.4 shows the property price indexes with the land and structure price indexes generated using DS2. The large fluctuations in land price indexes occur mostly in periods when property price and the exogenous construction cost move in opposite directions, such as the 4th quarter in 2005 and the 1st quarter in 2008.

The use of NDOPI as the structure price index in the DS models is adopted to deal with multicollinearity problems. Using the same approach, we can utilize exogenous information on land price and derive the structure prices from the DS models. The time-varying parameter $w_{L,t}$ now is set to be $w_L P_{L_t}$, proportional to some land price index, and the structure price

[4]In all DS models, the structure price indexes are equal to the construction cost index (NDOPI), thus we only use DS0 as a representation.

Table 8.6: Structure Price Indexes Comparison with Exogenous Land Price

Period	DS0	DS1	DS2	COLS	TD	SFA
1	1.0000	1.0000	1.0000	1.0000	1.0000	1.0000
2	1.0585	1.0509	1.0519	1.0470	1.0466	1.0470
3	1.0964	1.0973	1.1027	1.1095	1.1075	1.1095
4	1.0572	1.0641	1.0664	1.0648	1.0636	1.0648
5	1.0725	1.0686	1.0854	1.0747	1.0734	1.0747
6	1.0985	1.0872	1.0866	1.0612	1.0603	1.0612
7	1.1252	1.1232	1.1243	1.1023	1.1004	1.1023
8	1.0862	1.0859	1.0839	1.0865	1.0846	1.0865
9	1.0990	1.0910	1.0776	1.0985	1.0972	1.0985
10	1.1163	1.1144	1.1097	1.1505	1.1482	1.1505
11	1.1466	1.1494	1.1468	1.1632	1.1602	1.1632
12	1.1172	1.1189	1.1164	1.1263	1.1243	1.1263
13	1.0988	1.0925	1.0829	1.1126	1.1114	1.1126
14	1.1175	1.1156	1.1111	1.1268	1.1251	1.1268

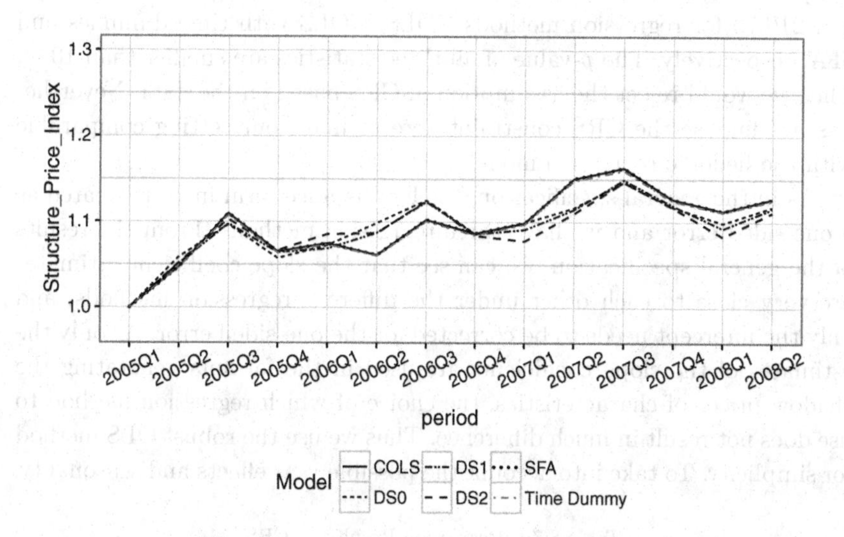

Fig. 8.5: Structure Price Index Comparison with Exogenous Land Price

parameter $w_{S,t}$ is allowed to freely change over each period. With all other settings remaining the same, we still denote the models as DS0, DS1 and DS2. The exogenous land price index is chosen to be the one generated from our model with time dummies. The resulting structure price indexes are shown in Table 8.6 and plotted in Figure 8.5. We can see that with the land price index derived from our model as exogenous information, the structure price indexes generated from the DS models show basically the same trend as our structure price indexes. Thus, the reliability of land or structure prices generated using the DS models heavily depends on how well the exogenous information reflects the true changing pattern of the price of the other component. The method we propose here can avoid the problem of multicollinearity in hedonic regression and construct the land and structure price indexes at the same time. Our methods also tend to smooth the price fluctuations and are less sensitive to market changes compared to the DS models.

8.4.3 *Specification with constant-returns-to-scale assumption*

Compared with the general specification, the setting under the *CRS* assumption is a constrained regression with $\alpha_{11} = \gamma_1 = \gamma_2 = 0$. We conduct the joint F-test for these constraints, and the F-statistics are 59.7, 67.16 and 216.79 for regression methods COLS, COLS with time dummies and SFA, respectively. The p-value of all three statistics are smaller than 10^{-4}. Thus we would reject the assumption of CRS based on the data. Nevertheless, we impose the CRS constraint here to make our setting comparable with the hedonic regression model.

As in the general specification, the log-distance term $\ln D_i$ is treated as a one-sided error and we have three regression methods. From the results of the general specification, we can see that the slope coefficient estimates are very close to each other under the different regression methods, and only the intercept needs to be corrected for the one-sided error. As only the estimates of the slope coefficients are used in the formula generating the shadow prices of characteristics, the choice of which regression method to use does not result in much difference. Thus we use the robust OLS method for simplicity. To take into account the possible year effects and seasonality,

Table 8.7: Regression Results — CRS

	Coef.	Std. err.	t
cons	−0.257646	0.114862	−2.24
$\ln(S/A)$	0.9153355	0.075584	12.11
$\ln(L/A)$	0.1219993	0.0539718	2.26
$(\ln(S/A))^2$	−0.018214	0.0189258	−0.96
$(\ln(L/A))^2$	0.029778	0.0107326	2.77
$\ln(S/A)\ln(L/A)$	−0.000395	0.0241278	−0.02

Table 8.8: Price Indexes Comparison with CRS

Structure price indexes comparison with CRS			Land price indexes comparison with CRS		
TD-CRS	TD	Diewert	TD-CRS	TD	Diewert
1.0000	1.0000	1.0000	1.0000	1.0000	1.0000
1.0439	1.0466	0.9929	1.0242	1.0263	1.1386
1.0940	1.1075	1.0152	1.0185	1.0191	1.1653
1.0562	1.0636	1.0395	0.9991	0.9975	1.0421
1.0646	1.0734	1.0071	1.0156	1.0147	1.1189
1.0521	1.0603	1.0172	1.0482	1.0507	1.1818
1.0853	1.1004	1.0122	1.0574	1.0602	1.2350
1.0698	1.0846	1.0152	1.0425	1.0445	1.1326
1.0840	1.0972	1.0344	1.0889	1.0967	1.2120
1.1291	1.1482	1.0445	1.0715	1.0770	1.1955
1.1368	1.1602	1.0688	1.0719	1.0759	1.1775
1.1061	1.1243	1.0921	1.0783	1.0833	1.1159
1.0991	1.1114	1.1134	1.0710	1.0774	1.0507
1.1094	1.1251	1.1134	1.0834	1.0916	1.0965

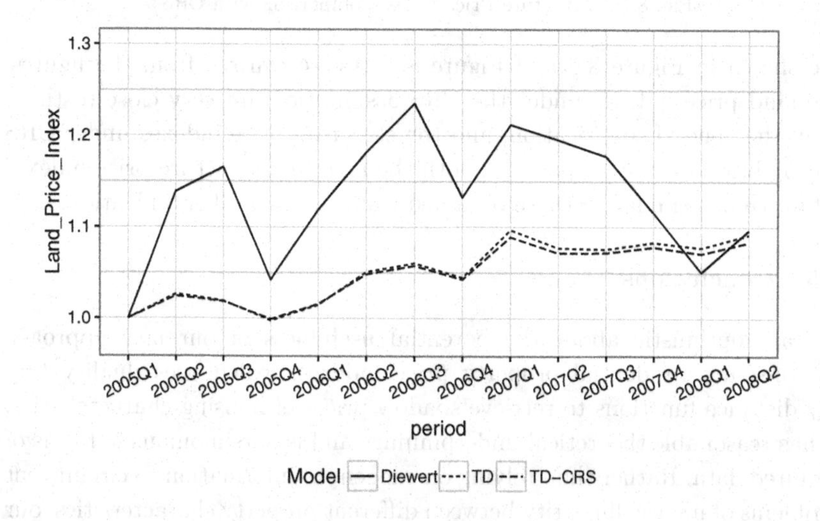

Fig. 8.6: Land Price Index Comparison with CRS

we include dummies for both years and quarters in our regression. The estimation results are shown in Table 8.7. Using formulas (8.27), we can then construct the price indexes of structure and land, which are shown in Table 8.8. As we add dummies to pick up the yearly and quarterly effects in the regression, we compare the results under the CRS assumption with those obtained in the general specification with time dummy variables, and denote these as TD-CRS and TD correspondingly. The plots of the indexes

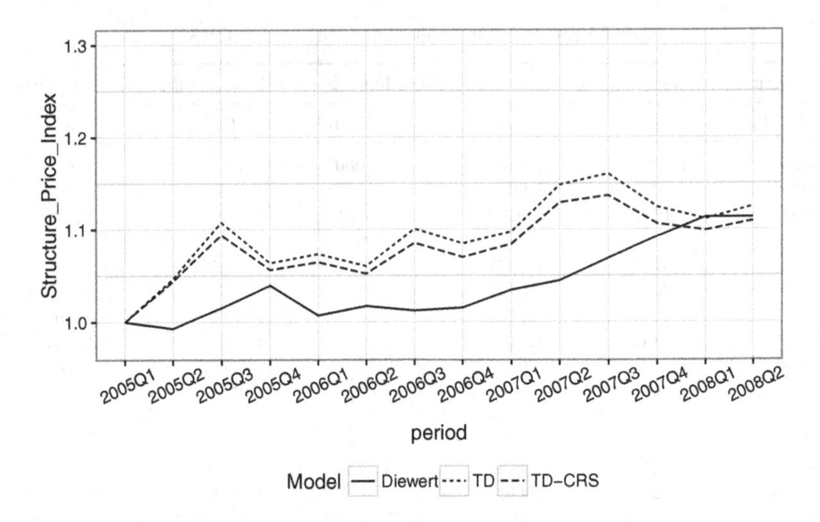

Fig. 8.7: Structure Price Index Comparison with CRS

are shown in Figure 8.6 and Figure 8.7. As we can see from the figures, the land price indexes under the CRS assumption are very close to those from the general specification, and the structure price indexes under CRS are slightly lower in all periods. Both the land and structure price indexes retain trends similar to those obtained from the general specification.

8.5 Conclusions

We are optimistic about the potential usefulness of our new approach to construct residential property price indexes, which uses duality theory distance functions to retrieve shadow prices of housing characteristics. It has reasonable theoretical underpinnings and is parsimonious in terms of required data. Rather than relying on exogenous information to circumvent problems of multicollinearity between different property characteristics, our method can estimate the shadow price of each characteristic with little computational burden. As this model is less sensitive to actual market fluctuations, it also can be combined with traditional hedonic regression methods to provide bounds on residential property prices based on mark-to-market adjustment and less volatile consumer preferences.

Chapter 9

Shadow Price Estimates of Wetlands in the St. John's Bayou–New Madrid Floodway

William L. Weber

9.1 Introduction

The Great Mississippi Flood of 1927 left 313 people dead, inundated 18 million acres of land, caused $300 million[1] in damage (Hoyt and Langbein, 1955) and led to passage of the Flood Control Act of 1928. Much of the 3700 miles of levees along the Mississippi, Arkansas and Red Rivers was built and is maintained by the Army Corps of Engineers. Cairo, Illinois sits about a mile north of the confluence of the Ohio and Mississippi Rivers. Directly across from Cairo is the Birds Point–New Madrid Floodway located in Southeast Missouri. Beginning at Birds Point, the 130,000 acre Floodway is encompassed by a front-line levee adjacent to the Mississippi River and a setback levee between three and ten miles west of the frontline levee. The levees extend southward approximately 30 miles to New Madrid where a 1500 foot gap prevents the meeting of the two levees and provides a link with the land and the river. The St. John's Bayou extends to the northwest

[1]In 1950 real dollars, as reported by Hoyt and Langbein (1955). For comparison, the CPIs in 1927, 1950 and 2017 are 17.4, 24.1 and 244.08, respectively.
Source: www.bls.gov/cpi/tables/historical-cpi-u-201709.pdf.

of the setback levee. Locally heavy rain events cause water to overflow ditches and pool along the setback levee when the floodgates are closed.

As designed, the 1500 foot gap in the levees is complemented with a northern fuse plug section that is to be blown by dynamite during extreme Mississippi flooding. Upon activation up to 550,000 cubic feet of water per second can flow through the Floodway and reduce the water level at Cairo by up to 7 feet. The fuse plug levee has been activated only twice — once in 1937 and most recently in 2011. The Army Corps of Engineers has been a proponent of closing the gap in the Floodway ever since the 1954 Flood Control Act authorized its closing. In addition, the Corps also proposed the installation of pumps to alleviate the sump area in the Bayou. However, environmental groups, the U.S. Fish and Wildlife Agency and the Environmental Protection Agency oppose the Corps' plan based on lost wetland habitat in the Floodway and St. John's Bayou.

In this chapter, a shadow pricing model is used to estimate the environmental benefits of the wetlands formed by the St. John's Bayou and New Madrid Floodway in Southeast Missouri. Maintaining and preventing the conversion of wetlands to alternative uses such as agriculture imposes an opportunity cost — economic value in such uses is foregone. The model estimates the shadow price of an acre of wetlands as the value of lost agricultural output. Data from 51 counties in five states — Missouri, Illinois, Kentucky, Tennessee and Arkansas — surrounding the New Madrid Floodway and St. John's Bayou are used to estimate the shadow price of wetlands.[2] Figure 9.1 shows the geographic region of the 51 counties.

9.2 Levees and Wetlands

Although the preservation and enhancement of wetlands guide wetland policy today, The Swampland Acts of 1849, 1850 and 1860 gave more than 64.9 million acres to the states to reclaim wetlands via the construction of levees and ditches. The Army Corps of Engineers began flood control work on the Mississippi River system in the 1870s and approximately 800,000 acres of wetlands were lost annually before 1954. From the mid-1950s to the mid-1970s various policies slowed the reduction of wetlands, and in recent years the conversion halted as some wetlands were restored.

[2]Weber (2015) provides additional information on the 1928 Flood Control Act, wetlands and the Mississippi levee system.

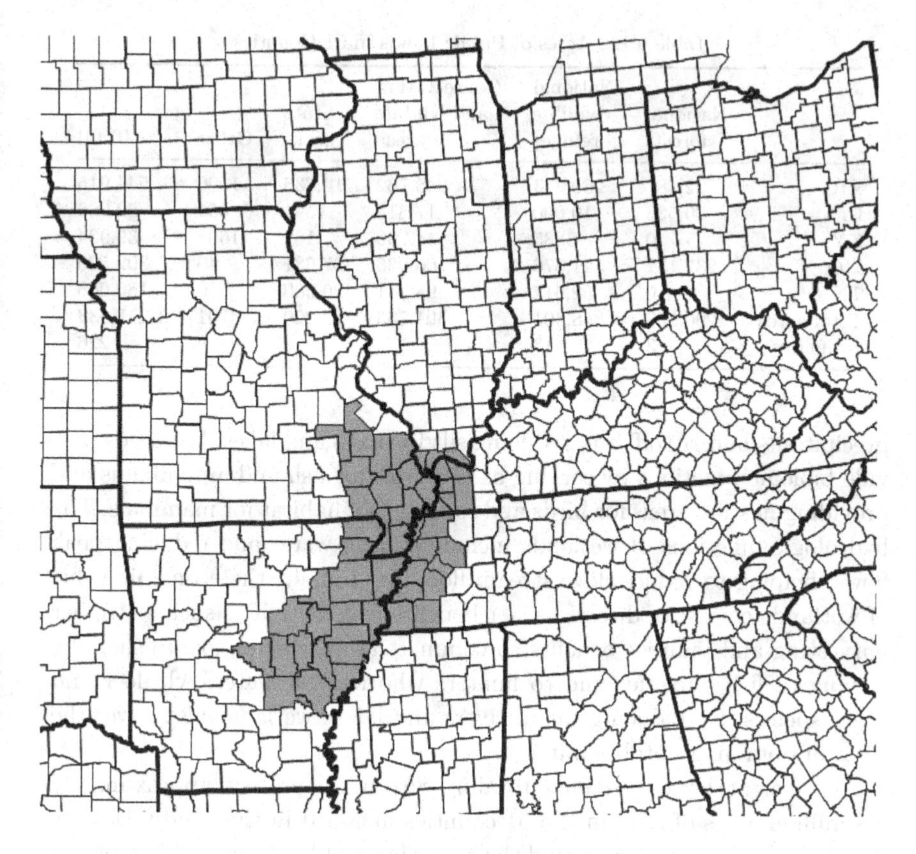

Fig. 9.1: Region of Study

According to the Mississippi River Commission and the US Army Corps of Engineers, the most important levee in the lower Mississippi basin is the Commerce to Birds Point mainline levee which connects with the setback levee at Birds Point. Starting at Commerce, Missouri this levee protects 1 million acres of prime agricultural bottom land in Missouri and Arkansas and approximately 2.5 million acres in total (Camillo, 2012; Olson and Morton, 2013). Without this levee the Mississippi River would cut a swath into the 40 mile wide and 200 mile long St. Francis River basin and not return to the main branch of the Mississippi River until the mouth of the St. Francis, below Memphis and about seven miles above Helena, Arkansas Wetlands provide numerous functions: ecologic, biologic, hydrologic and economic (Heimlich *et al.*, 1998). The ecological functions of wetlands include absorbing sediment from decaying plant matter, serving as a sponge for chemical

Table 9.1: Acres of Public Lands in 51 Counties

	National forests	National wildlife refuges	Conservation and wildlife areas	State parks	Other	Total
AR	22,687	260,223	245,762	14,736	1506	544,915
IL	30,533	10,000	17,318	1591	554	59,996
KY	0	3885	34,266	182	1601	39,934
MO	237,137	21,676	106,036	27,631	40	392,520
TN	0	52,617	98,371	29,080	0	180,068
Total acres	290,357	348,401	501,753	73,220	3701	1,217,433
# of sites	3	13	173	28	9	226

precipitants and runoff, and reducing silt in rivers and lakes. Wetlands provide biologic functions by serving as estuaries for fish and amphibians and providing nesting areas for birds and serving as a habitat for mammals. The hydrologic functions of wetlands include storing water and reducing peak flows, helping to reduce downstream flooding. Finally, the economic value of wetlands consist of direct market benefits from activities such as timber harvesting and indirect benefits to commercial and recreational fishers by serving as fish nurseries and to hunters who harvest waterfowl, deer and other species. By reducing silt in rivers and lakes, wetlands also lower the costs of obtaining potable water.

Sixty-eight levee segments totaling 891 miles protect approximately 2.8 million acres of land in the 51 counties included in this study. Despite the levee system the area around the New Madrid Floodway is rich in public lands, many of which are wetlands. Table 9.1 reports the total number of acres and the number of different kinds of public land sites in the 51 counties. Thirteen national wildlife refuges, 3 national forests, 28 state parks, 73 state conservation and wildlife management areas, and 9 other public sites provide 1.2 million acres of land for wildlife habitat and recreational opportunities.

9.3 A Shadow Pricing Model for Public Lands

9.3.1 *Theory*

Public lands tend to be non-market outputs so their values must be obtained indirectly. To obtain prices for public lands — which we then use to price wetlands in the New Madrid Floodway — we specify a production technology and use the directional output distance function as a functional representation of that technology. We exploit the duality between the revenue function and the directional output distance function to obtain shadow prices of the non-market outputs (Färe, Grosskopf and Weber, 2001). The shadow price of the non-market output represents its opportunity cost in terms of the value of foregone production of a marketed output.

We assume a set of $k = 1, \ldots, K$ producers employ $x = (x_1, \ldots, x_N)$ inputs to produce $y = (y_1, \ldots, y_M)$ outputs. The output possibility set gives the set of outputs that can be produced with given inputs and is represented as

$$P(x) = \{y : x \text{ can produce } y\}. \tag{9.1}$$

We assume that $P(x)$ is convex with inputs and outputs strongly disposable. The directional output distance function serves as a functional representation of the output possibility set. This function was developed by Chambers, Chung and Färe (1996, 1998) who adapted Luenberger's (1992) consumer benefit function for use in production theory. Let $g = (g_1, \ldots, g_M)$ represent a directional vector or path along which outputs are projected to the frontier of $P(x)$. The directional output distance function takes the form

$$\vec{D}_o(x, y; g) = \max\{\beta : y + \beta \times g \in P(x)\}. \tag{9.2}$$

The product of $\vec{D}_o(x, y; g)$ and g gives the maximum addition to each output that can be feasibly produced given inputs and the technology. The distance function, $\vec{D}_o(x, y; g)$, serves as a measure of inefficiency. If $\vec{D}_o(x, y; g) = 0$, a given (x, y) combination is efficient; outputs cannot be feasibly increased given inputs. Inefficient producers have $\vec{D}_o(x, y; g) > 0$, with larger values indicating greater inefficiency.

The directional vector determines how outputs are scaled to the frontier. For example, when a directional vector of $g = (1, 1, \ldots, 1)$ is chosen, $\vec{D}_o(x, y; g)$ gives the maximum unit expansion in all outputs. When a directional vector of $g = (1, 0, 0, \ldots, 0)$ is chosen $\vec{D}_o(x, y; g)$ gives the maximum unit expansion y_1, other outputs held constant. A special case occurs when a directional vector of $g = (y_1, \ldots, y_M)$ is chosen. Here, $\vec{D}_o(x, y; g)$ multiplied by 100% gives the maximum percentage expansion in all outputs.

The directional output distance function completely characterizes the production technology in that

$$y \in P(x) \Longleftrightarrow \vec{D}_o(x, y; g) \geq 0. \tag{9.3}$$

The properties of the directional output distance function are inherited from the production technology. For $y \in P(x)$ these properties are

$$\begin{aligned} &\text{(i) } \vec{D}_o(x, y; g) \geq 0 \\ &\text{(ii) } y' \leq y, \vec{D}_o(x, y'; g) \geq \vec{D}_o(x, y; g) \\ &\text{(iii) } x' \geq x, \vec{D}_o(x', y; g) \geq \vec{D}_o(x, y; g). \end{aligned} \tag{9.4}$$

Property 9.4(i) is the feasibility property. Properties 9.4(ii and iii) impose a monotonicity condition on outputs and inputs. If a firm produces more outputs given inputs its inefficiency will not increase, and if a firm uses more inputs to produce given outputs its inefficiency will not decrease. The directional distance function also has the translation property which is an additive representation of the technology, similar to the homogeneity property of Shephard output distance functions. The translation property follows from the definition of $\vec{D}_o(x, y; g)$ and is given as

$$\vec{D}_o(x, y + \alpha \times g; g) = \vec{D}_o(x, y; g) - \alpha. \tag{9.5}$$

To derive shadow prices for the non-market outputs we exploit the duality between the directional output distance function and the revenue function. Let $p = (p_1, \ldots, p_M)$ represent a vector of output prices. The revenue function is defined as

$$R(x, p) = \max_y \{py : y \in P(x)\}, \tag{9.6}$$

or by the representation property

$$R(x, p) = \max_y \{py : \vec{D}_o(x, y; g) \geq 0\}. \tag{9.7}$$

The revenue function gives the maximum revenue for feasible output vectors, and since $y + \vec{D}_o(x, y; g)g$ is a feasible output vector we can write

$$R(x, p) \geq py + p\vec{D}_o(x, y; g)g. \tag{9.8}$$

The inequality in (9.8) derives from the fact that once outputs are scaled to the frontier and all technical inefficiency is eliminated, revenues associated with the frontier outputs $(py + p\vec{D}_o(x, y; g)g)$ might still be less than the maximum because the frontier outputs are not allocatively efficient.

Rearranging (9.8) yields

$$\vec{D}_o(x, y; g) \leq \frac{R(x,p) - py}{pg}. \tag{9.9}$$

The directional output distance function can be recovered from the revenue function as

$$\vec{D}_o(x, y; g) = \min_p \frac{R(x,p) - py}{pg}. \tag{9.10}$$

Taking the gradient function of (9.10) with respect to outputs yields

$$\nabla_y \vec{D}_o(x, y; g) = \frac{-p}{pg} \tag{9.11}$$

and given two outputs, y_m and y_j, the shadow price of y_m can be recovered as

$$p_m = p_j \frac{\partial \vec{D}_o(x, y; g)/\partial y_m}{\partial \vec{D}_o(x, y; g)/\partial y_j}. \tag{9.12}$$

The directional output distance function projects a producer's outputs to the frontier. The slope of the frontier at the point of projection equals the marginal rate of transformation between the two outputs, i.e., the physical opportunity cost of producing one more unit of output m in terms of foregone output j. In (9.12) the term $\frac{\partial \vec{D}_o(x,y;g)/\partial y_m}{\partial \vec{D}_o(x,y;g)/\partial y_j}$ represents the marginal rate of transformation Thus, if the jth price is known and the marginal rate of transformation is estimated, the shadow price of output m can be obtained.

9.3.2 *Functional form*

To operationalize the shadow pricing formula given by (9.12) we follow Chambers' (1998) suggestion and use a quadratic form for the directional output distance function. The quadratic serves as a second-order approximation to the true, but unknown function, and the parameters can be restricted to satisfy the monotonicity properties given by (9.4) and the translation property given by (9.5).

The quadratic directional output distance function is given as

$$\vec{D}_o(x,y;g) = \alpha_0 + \sum_{m=1}^{M} \alpha_m y_m + \sum_{n=1}^{N} \beta_n x_n + \frac{1}{2}\sum_{m=1}^{M}\sum_{m'=1}^{M} \alpha_{mm'} y_m y_{m'}$$

$$+ \frac{1}{2}\sum_{n=1}^{N}\sum_{n'=1}^{N} \beta_{nn'} x_n x_{n'} + \sum_{m=1}^{M}\sum_{n=1}^{N} \delta_{mn} y_m x_n + \sum_{t=2}^{T} \gamma_t DT_t. \tag{9.13}$$

Symmetry restrictions for the cross-output and cross-input effects are imposed so that $\alpha_{mm'} = \alpha_{m'm}$ and $\beta_{nn'} = \beta_{n'n}$. The translation property requires that $\sum_{m=1}^{M} \alpha_m g_m = -1$, $\sum_{m'=1}^{M} \alpha_{mm'} g_m = 0, m = 1, \ldots, M$, and $\sum_{m=1}^{M} \delta_{mn} g_m = 0, n = 1, \ldots, N$ (Hudgins and Primont, 2007). Included in (9.13) are time indicator variables, DT_t, that allow the production frontier to shift from period to period due to exogenous events, such as weather and flooding.

To estimate (9.13) we follow Aigner and Chu (1968) and estimate a deterministic directional output distance function using linear programming. This method minimizes the sum of the distances of each producer's observed outputs to the frontier outputs. Recall that $\vec{D}_o(x,y;g) = 0$ when a producer is on the frontier. Given $k = 1, \ldots, K$ producers we choose α_0, α_m, $\alpha_{mm'}$, β_n, $\beta_{nn'}$, δ_{mn} and γ_t to

$$\sum_{t=1}^{T}\sum_{k=1}^{K} \vec{D}_o(x_k^t, y_k^t; g) - 0 \text{ subject to}$$

(i) $\vec{D}_o(x_k^t, y_k^t; g) \geq 0, k = 1, \ldots, K, t = 1, \ldots, T$

(ii) $\partial\vec{D}_o(x_k^t, y_k^t; g)/\partial y_{km}^t \leq 0, m = 1, \ldots, M, k = 1, \ldots, K, t = 1, \ldots, T$

(iii) $\partial\vec{D}_o(x_k^t, y_k^t; g)/\partial x_{kn}^t \geq 0, n = 1, \ldots, N, k = 1, \ldots, K, t = 1, \ldots, T$

(iv) $\alpha_{mm'} = \alpha_{m'm}, \beta_{nn'} = \beta_{n'n}$

(v) $\sum_{m=1}^{M} \alpha_m g_m = -1, \sum_{m'=1}^{M} \alpha_{mm'} g_m = 0, m = 1, \ldots, M$ and

$$\sum_{m=1}^{M} \delta_{mn} g_m = 0, n = 1, \ldots, N. \tag{9.14}$$

The restrictions given by (9.14i) require that the observed outputs and inputs be feasible for every observation in each year. The restrictions in

(9.14ii) and (9.14iii) impose the monotonicity conditions for outputs and inputs, i.e., disposability. Symmetry conditions for the cross-output and cross-input effects are imposed by (9.14iv). Finally, the restrictions associated with the translation property are imposed by (9.14v).

Although different directional vectors can be chosen, they need to be common for all observations to avoid having to parameterize the directional vectors in the quadratic form.

9.4 Data

To implement the shadow pricing model we employ pooled data on 51 counties located in five states during 2009–2012. We assume that public lands would be employed in agriculture in their next best alternative so each county's agricultural output is used as the private good. Agricultural output (y_1) equals the inflation-adjusted (base year $=$ 1984) value of crop revenues derived from corn, soybeans, wheat, cotton and rice. We sum acres of National Forest land and National Wildlife Refuges in each county to get federal land acres (y_2) and the acres that are state parks, wildlife management acres or other state lands to get state land acres (y_3). The inputs are farm employment (x_1), real farm expenditures on lime, fertilizer, and pesticides (x_2), real farm expenditures on petroleum and other expenses (x_3), and the number of square miles in the county. Crop revenues, farm labor and farm expenditures for fertilizer and petroleum and other farm expenditures vary by year. The number of square miles in the county, and the number of acres of federal land and state land are constant for the 4 years.

The average number of square miles in a county is 561 (358,940 acres), with less than 10% of that area (23,872 acres) devoted to public lands consisting of 12,525 acres of federal land in the form of National Wildlife Refuges or National Forests and 11,347 acres of state lands in the form of wildlife management areas, state parks or other state lands. The average county employs 648 farm workers and uses \$11.3 million in fertilizer and \$22.8 million in petroleum and other farm expenditures to generate real crop revenues of \$903.5 million.

To estimate (9.14) a directional vector must be chosen which will determine the projection of observed outputs to the production frontier and the slope of the frontier at the projected point. Two alternative directional vectors corresponding to $g = (1, 1, 1)$ and $g = (0, 1, 1)$ are chosen to illustrate. Each directional vector influences the parameter estimates reported

Table 9.2: Parameter Estimates for $\vec{D}_o(x, y; g)$

Parm.	Variable	$g = (1,1,1)$ Estimate	$g = (0,1,1)$ Estimate
α_0	constant	3.395	19.781
α_1	y_1	−0.690	−0.911
α_2	y_2	−0.159	−0.702
α_3	y_3	−0.151	−0.298
β_1	x_1	6.089	10.634
β_2	x_2	1.182	2.162
β_3	x_3	0.394	0.000
β_4	x_4	−2.180	1.346
α_{11}	y_1^2	0.011	0.012
α_{12}	y_1y_2	−0.005	0.005
α_{13}	y_1y_3	−0.006	−0.005
α_{22}	y_2^2	0.002	0.002
α_{23}	y_2y_3	0.003	−0.002
α_{33}	y_3^2	0.003	0.002
β_{11}	x_1^2	−1.631	0.024
β_{12}	x_1x_2	0.436	−1.355
β_{13}	x_1x_3	−0.059	0.000
β_{14}	x_1x_4	−1.528	−9.537
β_{22}	x_2^2	0.101	−0.030
β_{23}	x_2x_3	−0.006	0.000
β_{24}	x_2x_4	0.257	4.350
β_{33}	x_3^2	−0.004	0.000
β_{34}	x_3x_4	−0.114	0.000
β_{44}	x_4^2	6.652	17.176
δ_{11}	y_1x_1	−0.074	0.420
δ_{12}	y_1x_2	−0.040	−0.026
δ_{13}	y_1x_3	0.002	0.000
δ_{14}	y_1x_4	0.340	−0.527
δ_{21}	y_2x_1	0.180	0.158
δ_{22}	y_2x_2	0.022	−0.014
δ_{23}	y_2x_3	−0.001	0.000
δ_{24}	y_2x_4	−0.346	0.327
δ_{31}	y_3x_1	−0.106	−0.158
δ_{32}	y_3x_2	0.018	−0.014
δ_{33}	y_3x_3	−0.001	0.000
δ_{34}	y_3x_4	0.006	−0.327
γ_2	$t = 2010$	0.725	0.594
γ_3	$t = 2011$	−0.341	−0.242
γ_4	$t = 2012$	0.438	−2.506

in Table 9.2 through the restrictions implied by the translation property in (9.14v).

All outputs and inputs were divided by 1000 before estimating. For the $g = (1, 1, 1)$ estimates the time effects, γ_2 and γ_4, are positive indicating

Table 9.3: Estimates of Inefficiency

	2009	2010	2011	2012	All years
$g = (1, 1, 1)$					
$\vec{D}_o(x, y; g)$	5.93	6.03	5.11	7.25	6.08
# on frontier	3	2	5	4	14
$g = (0, 1, 1)$					
$\vec{D}_o(x, y; g)$	14.71	14.22	13.20	11.94	13.52
# on frontier	2	2	3	7	14

that the frontier shifted to the Northeast in 2010 and 2012 relative to 2009. Such a shift might be due to technological progress or better growing conditions in 2010 and 2012 relative to 2009. However, γ_3 is negative indicating an inward shift in the production frontier in 2011. Such an inward shift is consistent with the high water during the spring of 2011 when farmers in the Floodway (and in other areas) lost the winter wheat crop due to flooding. In addition, wet conditions which delayed planting probably caused some farmers to plant soybeans rather than corn, resulting in lost revenues. A similar pattern holds for the $g = (0, 1, 1)$ estimates except now γ_4 is negative.

Table 9.3 reports the estimates of the directional output distance function and the number of frontier counties for the two directional vectors. For the directional vector $g = (1, 1, 1)$, inefficiency averages 6.08 for the pooled sample; if the average county were to produce on the best-practice production frontier state and federal lands could each each increase by 6080 acres and county farm income could increase by \$6.08 million. The number of frontier counties ranged from two in 2010 to five in 2011, with a total of 14 counties defining the production frontier. Production among the 51 counties exhibited the least inefficiency in 2011 and the most inefficiency in 2012.

Relative to the directional vector that seeks the expansion in real crop revenues and federal and state lands, $g = (1, 1, 1)$, inefficiency is greater for the directional vector that holds crop revenues constant and expands federal and state land acres, $(g = (0, 1, 1))$.

The shadow price estimates for federal $(\hat{p}_2)$ and state lands $(\hat{p}_3)$ are reported in Table 9.4 for various directional vectors. These shadow price estimates are derived from (9.12) using the parameter estimates reported in Table 9.2. We use the real price of crop revenues as the known market price, with $p_1 = 1$. The shadow prices for federal lands $(\hat{p}_2)$ and state lands

Table 9.4: Mean Shadow Price Estimates for Public Lands[a]

	2009	2010	2011	2012	All years
$g = (1, 1, 1)$					
Federal lands $= \hat{p}_2$	411.0	484.7	490.4	397.2	445.8
State lands $= \hat{p}_3$	553.7	650.6	664.2	548.4	604.2
$g = (0, 1, 1)$					
Federal lands $= \hat{p}_2$	504.2	505.6	519.5	524.3	513.4
State lands $= \hat{p}_3$	1067.3	1133.3	1216.1	1095.4	1128.0

[a]Shadow prices are in 1984 dollars per acre.

($\hat{p}_3$) are estimated as

$$p_m = p_1 \left(\frac{\alpha_1 + \sum_{m'=1}^{M} \alpha_{1m'} y_{m'} + \sum_{n=1}^{N} \delta_{1n} x_n}{\alpha_m + \sum_{m'=1}^{M} \alpha_{mm'} y_{m'} + \sum_{n=1}^{N} \delta_{mn} x_n} \right), \quad m = 2, 3. \tag{9.15}$$

All shadow price estimates are in 1984 dollars, but can be converted to 2015 dollars by multiplying by the 2015 mid-year CPI of 237 and dividing the result by 100. The directional vector $g = (1, 1, 1)$ generated a shadow price of federal lands equal to \$445.8 and a shadow price for state lands equal to \$604.2. When $g = (0, 1, 1)$ the shadow price of federal lands increases to \$513.4 and the shadow price of state lands increases to \$1128.

9.4.1 *Using the model to value wetlands in the New Madrid floodway and St. John's Bayou*

Table 9.5 reports details on the outputs and inputs for Mississippi and New Madrid counties, home to the St. John's Bayou and New Madrid Floodway. Mississippi county has 6,446 acres of state lands and zero federal lands. New Madrid county has 6,322 acres of state lands and zero federal lands. New Madrid county has greater real crop revenues, partly attributable to a larger land area — 678 square miles in New Madrid county vs 413 square miles in Mississippi county. Crop revenues increased from 2009 to 2012, but the gap between the two counties was greatest in 2011 when New Madrid county produced 82% more real crop revenues than Mississippi county. However, despite the larger farm output, New Madrid county was less efficient than Mississippi county in each of the 4 years. In fact, Mississippi county was one of the frontier counties in 2012 and exhibited lower inefficiency on average than the other counties in the study (see Table 9.3). In contrast, New Madrid county exhibited greater inefficiency in each of the 4 years than the average inefficiency of the other counties in the study.

Table 9.5: Outputs, Inefficiency and Shadow Prices of Public Lands in Mississippi and New Madrid Counties: $g = (1, 1, 1)$

Year	Real farm income (1000s)	$\vec{D}_o(x, y; g)$	Shadow price[a] of Federal lands $= \hat{p}_2$	State lands $= \hat{p}_3$
Mississippi County				
2009	55,593	2.92	508	634
2010	57,988	1.31	667	814
2011	59,531	3.45	403	546
2012	73,434	0	576	806
New Madrid County				
2009	82,614	12.42	463	626
2010	96,982	6.90	1117	1440
2011	108,531	5.19	731	1063
2012	105,776	14.42	178	417

[a]Shadow prices are in 1984 dollars.

Frontier output is $y^* = (y + \beta^* g)$, where β^* equals the estimate of the directional output distance function, $\vec{D}_o(x, y; g)$. Now, consider the data for 2009 for the two counties. If Mississippi county had realized greater inefficiency for the $g = (1, 1, 1)$ estimates an extra \$2.92 million in crop revenues, an extra 2920 acres of federal lands and an extra 2920 acres of state lands would have been produced resulting in frontier quantities of $y^* = (58{,}513, 2{,}920, 9{,}366)$. For those quantities, the shadow price of federal lands is \$508 and the shadow price of state lands in \$634. In New Madrid county, greater efficiency could have allowed real crop revenues to increase by \$12.42 million, federal lands to increase by 12,420 acres and state lands to increase by 12,420 acres giving $y^* = (95{,}034, 12{,}420, 18{,}742)$. Given those quantities the shadow price of an acre of federal land is \$463 and the shadow price of an extra acre of state land is \$626. The shadow prices vary by year as the quantities and mix of inputs — farm labor, fertilizer, and petroleum and other expenses — vary. The shadow prices have a smaller range for state lands in Mississippi county, \$546 to \$814, than in New Madrid county where the range is between \$178 and \$1440.

In Mississippi county the state lands include Big Oak Tree State Park (1000 acres), Seven Island Conservation Area (1381 acres) and Ten Mile Pond Conservation Area (3755 acres), all important wetland areas. Two of these areas (Big Oak Tree SP and Ten Mile Pond CA) lie within the Floodway, and Seven Island CA lies between the frontline levee and the

Mississippi River. In New Madrid county Donaldson Point CA (5785 acres) also lies between the frontline levee and the Mississippi River just east of the town of New Madrid. This area also consists of wetland and bottomland hardwoods.

According to the US Fish and Wildlife Service there are approximately 30,622 acres of wetlands in the St. John's Bayou basin and 36,883 acres of wetlands in the New Madrid Floodway (Ledwin and Roberts, 2000). Mississippi and New Madrid counties (of which the Bayou and Floodway are part) also have more diverse habitats and wildlife and fish species than other counties in the Missouri bootheel. Under the authorized Corps' plan wetlands would decline by almost 24,000 acres in the St. John's Bayou and by approximately 7,000 acres in the Floodway. Given only 6136 acres of public lands in Mississippi county and only 6322 acres of public lands in New Madrid county, much of the decline in wetlands would come on private property. Using the highest shadow price for wetlands in Mississippi county, \$814 for state lands in 2010, the 32,138 acres of wetlands currently located on private property are generating approximately \$26 million in value in 1984 dollars which converted to 2015 dollars equals \$61.6 million.[3] A lower bound estimate using the 2011 shadow price of \$403 for federal lands in Mississippi county yields approximately \$13 million in value in 1984 dollars or \$31 million in 2015 dollars.

Under the authorized Corps' plan the 31,000 acre decline in wetlands should be considered part of the cost for closing the 1500 foot gap in the levees encompassing the Floodway. These costs can be reasonably approximated using the range of shadow prices reported in Table 9.5. Using the high shadow price of \$814, the lost value of wetlands in Mississippi county is $814 \times 31{,}000 = \$25.23$ million in 1984 dollars. Using the high shadow price of \$1440 the lost value of wetlands would be $1440 \times 31000 = \$44.64$ million in New Madrid county. Lower-bound estimates can be similarly obtained. Converted to 2015 dollars the lost value of wetlands ranges between \$60 million to \$106 million if the Corps' plan is implemented.

[3]Private wetland acres in the Floodway are estimated as total wetland acres less state lands: $36{,}883 - (1000 + 3755) = 32{,}128$. The CPI for the first half of 2015 is 237.088 with a base = 100 in 1984.

Chapter 10

Pricing Inputs and Outputs in Banking Using Directional Distance Functions

Maryam Hasannasab and Dimitris Margaritis

10.1 Introduction

The financial meltdown of the last decade that began with the collapse of the US subprime mortgage market in 2007 and advanced into a massive global financial crisis following the collapse of Lehman Brothers in 2008 epitomized the twin perils of undercapitalized banks and non-performing loans. At the core of the crisis was cheap money driven by exceptionally loose Fed policy post 2001, lax regulation exemplified by the Securities and Exchange Commission decision to relax capital requirements for the five US major investment banks including Lehman Brothers in 2004, exuberance and, above all, badly priced risk culminated by the exponential growth of synthetic collateralized debt securities.

In this chapter, we take a fresh look at developments surrounding the crisis. Specifically, we set out to estimate the opportunity costs of equity capital and risky loans from the angle of bank efficiency focusing on US banks. We incorporate the banks' capital structure into a model of its technology, hence explicitly capturing the way banks production decisions influence their riskiness (see Hughes, Mester and Moon, 2001; Weyman-Jones, 2016). Inherent in risk-taking behavior is an assessment of the cost of bank equity that we expect to vary with the banks capital structure rather than kept fixed and invariant to it (Allen, Carletti and Marquez, 2015). Since we are also interested in pricing non-performing loans, we adopt a model of technology that allows for the production of good and bad outputs. Our main hypothesis is that undercapitalized and highly leveraged banks are more likely to face higher rather than a lower price of equity capital, a proposition that we subject to empirical testing. The tools that we use in our empirical analysis are the pricing rules developed in Chapter 5. We employ parametric forms of directional distance functions (DDFs) to obtain shadow prices of bank inputs and outputs. DDFs are particularly useful for our purposes since they readily model technology with good and bad outputs. We exploit cost minimization and revenue maximization as the optimization criteria to derive direct pricing rules that can be used to shadow price inputs and outputs along with information on input and output quantities.

We also obtain indirect or cross-over pricing rules exploiting profit maximization as the optimization criterion that allows us to shadow price both inputs and outputs simultaneously. We proceed to price inputs given knowledge of one output price, and price outputs given knowledge of one input price along with information on input and output quantities. The directional input distance function is parameterized using a quadratic functional form (see Chambers, 2002). Shadow prices for inputs are obtained by applying an input DDF, shadow prices for outputs using an output DDF, while we price inputs and outputs simultaneously by utilizing a non-oriented DDF.

We study samples of US Federal Deposit Insurance Corporation (FDIC) member banks during the period 2002 to 2016, which allows us to evaluate the main hypotheses of interest before, during and after the subprime crisis. Standard finance approaches estimate the cost of capital using asset-pricing models based on market prices (see Green, Lopez and Wang, 2003; Barnes and Lopez, 2006; King, 2009; Baker and Wurgler, 2013). Instead, we construct a measure of the cost of bank equity capital by exploiting the duality between the DDF and the profit function, and similarly the duality between input or output DDFs and cost or revenue functions, respectively. The shadow price of equity will equal the market price when the amount of equity minimizes cost, maximizes revenue or maximizes profit, recognizing that the shadow price will still provide a measure of opportunity cost even if the level of equity does not conform to any of these optimization objectives (Hughes, Mester and Moon, 2001). Since we no longer require market prices, our method can be used to estimate the cost of equity capital for both publicly listed and non-listed banks.

This chapter is organized as follows. Section 10.2 describes the methodology used to compute the efficiency measures and shadow prices for inputs and outputs. Section 10.3 describes the data and presents the empirical results. Section 10.4 concludes.

10.2 Methodology

10.2.1 *Parametric method*

Bank efficiency measures can be constructed using either non-parametric or parametric techniques (see the literature reviews by Berger and Humphrey, 1997; Berger and Mester, 2003; Berger, 2007; Fethi and Pasiouras, 2010). Parametric methods are more convenient for our purposes since our focus is on shadow pricing. Following the pioneering works of Aigner and Chu (1968) and Aigner, Lovell and Schmidt (1977), several studies have estimated production, cost, revenue or profit frontier models using parametric functional forms (see for example, Fukuyama and Weber, 2008; Koutsomanoli-Filippaki, Margaritis and Staikouras, 2009, for applications of parametric forms of DDFs in banking).

Parametric models may be deterministic as in Aigner and Chu (1968) or stochastic as in Aigner, Lovell and Schmidt (1977). Aigner and Chu (1968) propose to estimate the parameters of the frontier model via mathematical programming methods. In our context, this amounts to minimizing the sum of deviations of the distance function value from the frontier subject to the underlying technology constraints, which is a linear programming model. The method is appealing since it readily models the theoretical constraints imposed on the technology. In contrast, stochastic frontier methods cannot guarantee that such restrictions will be satisfied at all data points, albeit they offer other advantages.

The constraint conditions cover the feasibility, monotonicity, disposability, and translation properties of the DDF. While desirable inputs and outputs satisfy strong disposability, we assume that undesirable outputs (non-performing loans) and desirable outputs (loans, other earning assets) satisfy joint weak disposability, recognizing that reduction of undesirable outputs is costly. Equity capital is a quasi-fixed input, so it is fixed in the short-run but variable in the long-run, and its shadow price is not constrained to be positive. The latter is important in our context since it recognizes that negative shadow capital prices may be the result of extensive deleveraging (see Weyman-Jones, 2016). In addition, we require the functional form to be flexible, with interaction and second-order terms providing a second-order approximation to the true but unknown technology (see Färe and Sung, 1986), and with restrictions on the parameters to satisfy the translation property (see Hudgins and Primont, 2007). We assume that we observe inputs, good and bad outputs, $(x, y, b) \in \mathcal{R}^N \times \mathcal{R}^M \times \mathcal{R}^J$, and in addition, we assume that both input and output direction vectors $g^x = (g_1^x, \ldots, g_N^x), g^y = (g_1^y, \ldots, g_M^y), g^b = (g_1^b, \ldots, g_J^b)$ are given. We could have chosen the direction vector endogenously albeit at the expense of converting the optimization problem to a nonlinear program. The directional technology distance function is defined as

$$\vec{D}_T\,(x, y, b : g^x, g^y, g^b) = \max\{\beta : (x - \beta g^x, y + \beta g^y, b - \beta g^b) \in T\}.$$

This function satisfies the representation and translation properties, i.e.,

$$T = \{(x, y, b) : \vec{D}_T\,(x, y, b : g^x, g^y, g^b) \geq 0\},$$

$$\vec{D}_T\,(x - \alpha g^x, y + \alpha g^y, b - \alpha g^b : g^x, g^y, g^b) = \overrightarrow{D_T}(x, y, b : g^x, g^y, g^b) - \alpha.$$

We parameterize the DDF using a quadratic functional form

$$\begin{aligned}
\vec{D}_T\,(x, y, b; g^x, g^y, g^b) = {} & \alpha_0 + \sum_{n=1}^{N} \alpha_n x_n + \sum_{m=1}^{M} \beta_m y_m + \sum_{j=1}^{J} \gamma_j b_j \\
& + \frac{1}{2} \sum_{n=1}^{N} \sum_{n'=1}^{N} \alpha_{nn'} x_n x_{n'} + \frac{1}{2} \sum_{m=1}^{M} \sum_{m'=1}^{M} \beta_{mm'} y_m y_{m'} \\
& + \frac{1}{2} \sum_{j=1}^{J} \sum_{j'=1}^{J} \gamma_{jj'} b_j b_{j'} + \sum_{n=1}^{N} \sum_{m=1}^{M} \delta_{nm} x_n y_m \\
& + \sum_{n=1}^{N} \sum_{j=1}^{J} \nu_{nj} x_n b_j + \sum_{m=1}^{M} \sum_{j=1}^{J} \mu_{mj} y_m b_j.
\end{aligned}$$

The quadratic DDF is estimated by solving the following linear programming problem.

$$\min \quad \sum_{k=1}^{K} \vec{D}_T\,(x^k, y^k, b^k; g^x, g^y, g^b).$$

s.t.

$$(1)\ \vec{D}_T\,(x^k, y^k, b^k; g^x, g^y, g^b) \geqq 0, \quad \text{(feasibility)}$$

$$(2)\ \partial_{y_m}\, \vec{D}_T\,(x^k, y^k, b^k; g^x, g^y, g^b) \leqq 0 \quad \text{(monotonicity)}$$

$$\partial_{x_n}\, \vec{D}_T\,(x^k, y^k, b^k; g^x, g^y, g^b) \geqq 0 \quad \text{(monotonicity)}$$

$$\partial_{b_j}\, \vec{D}_T\,(x^k, y^k, b^k; g^x, g^y, g^b) \geqq 0, \quad \text{(monotonicity)}$$

$$(3)\ \alpha_{nn'} = \alpha_{n'n}, \beta_{mm'} = \beta_{m'm}, \gamma_{jj'} = \gamma_{j'j}. \quad \text{(symmetry)}$$

$$(4) - \sum_{n=1}^{N} \alpha_n g_n^x + \sum_{m=1}^{M} \beta_m g_m^y - \sum_{j=1}^{J} \gamma_j g_j^b = -1 \quad \textbf{(translation)}$$

$$- \sum_{n=1}^{N} \delta_{nm} g_n^x + \sum_{m'=1}^{M} \beta_{mm'} g_{m'}^y - \sum_{j=1}^{J} \mu_{mj} g_j^b = 0 \quad m = 1, \ldots, M$$

$$- \sum_{n=1}^{N} \nu_{nj} g_n^x + \sum_{m=1}^{M} \mu_{mj} g_m^y - \sum_{j'=1}^{J} \gamma_{jj'} g_{j'}^b = 0 \quad j = 1, \ldots, J$$

$$- \sum_{n'=1}^{N} \alpha_{nn'} g_{n'}^x + \sum_{m=1}^{M} \delta_{nm} g_m^y - \sum_{j=1}^{J} \nu_{nj} g_j^b = 0. \quad n = 1, \ldots, N$$

Note that

$$\partial_{x_n} \vec{D}_T\left(x^k, y^k, b^k\right) = \frac{\partial \vec{D}_T(x, y, b)}{\partial x_n}$$

$$= \alpha_n + \sum_{n=1}^{N} \alpha_{nn} x_n^k + \sum_{m=1}^{M} \delta_{nm} y_m^k + \sum_{j=1}^{J} \nu_{nj} b_j^k$$

$$\partial_{y_m} \vec{D}_T\left(x^k, y^k, b^k\right) = \frac{\partial \vec{D}_T(x, y, b)}{\partial y_m}$$

$$= \beta_m + \sum_{m=1}^{M} \beta_{mm} y_m^k + \sum_{n=1}^{N} \delta_{nm} x_n^k + \sum_{j=1}^{J} \mu_{mj} b_j^k$$

$$\partial_{b_j} \vec{D}_T\left(x^k, y^k, b^k\right) = \frac{\partial \vec{D}_T(x, y, b)}{\partial b_j}$$

$$= \gamma_j + \sum_{j=1}^{J} \gamma_{jj} b_j^k + \sum_{n=1}^{N} \nu_{nj} x_n^k + \sum_{m=1}^{M} \mu_{mj} y_m^k.$$

10.2.2 *Shadow pricing*

We use different pricing rules associated with different cost, revenue and profit objectives for banks. The pricing rule based on an input DDF is associated with cost minimization and requires either total cost or one of the input prices to be known. The pricing rule based on an output DDF is associated with revenue maximization and requires either total revenue or one of the output prices to be known. The pricing rule based on a non-oriented DDF is associated with profit maximization and requires one of the input or output prices to be known. Since we are mainly interested in pricing inputs and outputs for which we have no explicit pricing information (equity capital and non-performing loans), we compare their shadow prices with the actual and shadow price of the corresponding inputs (deposits and borrowed funds) and outputs (loans and leases).

We first show how to calculate shadow prices for inputs and outputs using a non-oriented DDF that simultaneously contracts inputs and expands outputs using a directional vector (g^x, g^y, g^b). We rely on profit maximization as the optimization criterion, which allows us to construct shadow prices for both inputs and outputs. Second, we construct input prices using an input DDF (D_I), with a directional vector defined as, $(g^x, 0, 0)$, which contracts inputs, holding outputs fixed. Third, we exploit revenue maximization as the optimization criterion to construct shadow prices for outputs, both desirable and undesirable, using an output DDF, (D_O), with a direction vector defined as, $(0, g^y, g^b)$, which expands desirable outputs and contracts undesirable output, given inputs.

Unlike debt such as deposits or other borrowed funds, equity carries no explicit cost, albeit bank shareholders expect to earn a return on their equity investment that represents a cost to the bank. Similarly, the pricing of provisions for loan losses is not straightforward, recognizing that monitoring of non-performing loans is costly and there is uncertainty about potential costs (distress and bankruptcy). We estimate shadow prices using prices of associated inputs and outputs. Since smaller banks may have lesser ability to diversify their activities, and they may face higher capital costs, we would like to see if there any differences between large and small banks. Similarly, we would like to know how capital costs or loan losses might vary in relation to other bank indicators. We set up the profit maximization Lagrangian problem as follows:

$$\max py - wx - rb - \mu \vec{D}_T (x, y, b, g^x, g^y, g^b),$$

where p, w, r are the prices for desirable outputs y, inputs (x), and undesirable outputs b, respectively, and μ is the Lagrangian multiplier (a measure of how much profit would increase if the optimization constraint was relaxed). The first-order conditions associated with the Lagrangian profit maximization problem are as follows:

$$\begin{aligned} p - \mu \nabla_y \vec{D}_T (x, y, b, g^x, g^y, g^b) &= 0 \\ -w - \mu \nabla_x \vec{D}_T (x, y, b, g^x, g^y, g^b) &= 0 \\ -r - \mu \nabla_b \vec{D}_T (x, y, b, g^x, g^y, g^b) &= 0\,. \end{aligned} \tag{10.1}$$

If one output price, say p_1, is known then we have

$$\mu = \frac{p_1}{\partial_{y_1} \vec{D}_T\left(x, y, b, g^x, g^y, g^b\right)}.$$

Then as shown in Chapter 5, this will yield estimates for other prices, $p_2, \ldots, p_M, r_1, \ldots, r_J, w_1, \ldots, w_N$ as:

$$\begin{aligned}
(w_1, \ldots, w_n) &= -\frac{p_1}{\partial_{y_1} \vec{D}_T\left(x, y, b, g^x, g^y, g^b\right)} \\
&\quad \times (\partial_{x_1} \vec{D}_T\left(x, y, b, g^x, g^y, g^b\right), \ldots, \partial_{x_N} \vec{D}_T\left(x, y, b, g^x, g^y, g^b\right)) \\
(p_2, \ldots, p_m) &= \frac{p_1}{\partial_{y_1} \vec{D}_T\left(x, y, b, g^x, g^y, g^b\right)} \\
&\quad \times (\partial_{y_2} \vec{D}_T\left(x, y, b, g^x, g^y, g^b\right), \ldots, \partial_{y_M} \vec{D}_T(x, y, b, g^x, g^y, g^b)) \\
(r_1, \ldots, r_J) &= -\frac{p_1}{\partial_{y_1} \vec{D}_T\left(x, y, b, g^x, g^y, g^b\right)} \\
&\quad \times (\partial_{b_1} \vec{D}_T\left(x, y, b, g^x, g^y, g^b\right), \ldots, \partial_{b_J} \vec{D}_T\left(x, y, b, g^x, g^y, g^b\right)).
\end{aligned}$$

Similarly, if one of the input prices, say w_1, is known then

$$\mu = -\frac{w_1}{\partial_{x_1} \vec{D}_T\left(x, y, b, g^x, g^y, g^b\right)}.$$

Hence, estimates of all other prices, $w_2, \ldots, w_N, p_2, \ldots, p_M, r_1, \ldots, r_J$ are obtained as follows:

$$\begin{aligned}
(w_2, \ldots, w_n) &= \frac{w_1}{\partial_{x_1} \vec{D}_T(x, y, b, g^x, g^y, g^b)} \\
&\quad \times (\partial_{x_2} \vec{D}_T\left(x, y, b, g^x, g^y, g^b\right), \ldots, \partial_{x_N} \vec{D}_T(x, y, b, g^x, g^y, g^b)) \\
(p_1, \ldots, p_M) &= -\frac{w_1}{\partial_{x_1} \vec{D}_T\left(x, y, b, g^x, g^y, g^b\right)} \\
&\quad \times (\partial_{y_1} \vec{D}_T\left(x, y, b, g^x, g^y, g^b\right), \ldots, \partial_{y_M} \vec{D}_T\left(x, y, b, g^x, g^y, g^b\right)) \\
(r_1, \ldots, r_J) &= -\frac{w_1}{\partial_{x_1} \vec{D}_T\left(x, y, b, g^x, g^y, g^b\right)} \\
&\quad \times (\partial_{b_1} \vec{D}_T\left(x, y, b, g^x, g^y, g^b\right), \ldots, \partial_{b_J} \vec{D}_T\left(x, y, b, g^x, g^y, g^b\right)).
\end{aligned}$$

From here, by altering the optimization criterion and rewriting the first-order conditions for cost minimization in lieu of profit maximization, $-w - \mu \nabla_x \vec{D}_I(x, y, b; g^x) = 0$, we can derive the input pricing rule as

$$(w_1, \ldots, w_N) = C \frac{(\partial_{x_1} \vec{D}_I(x, y, b, g^x), \ldots, \partial_{x_N} \vec{D}_I(x, y, b, g^x))}{\nabla_x \vec{D}_I(x, y, b, g^x) x},$$

where C is observed total cost. Similarly, applying the first-order conditions for revenue maximization,

$$p - \mu \nabla_y \vec{D}_O(x, y, b; g^y, g^b) = 0$$
$$-r - \mu \nabla_b \vec{D}_O(x, y, b; g^y, g^b) = 0,$$

we can obtain pricing rules for desirable and undesirable outputs as

$$(p_1, \ldots, p_M) = R \frac{(\partial_{y_1} \vec{D}_O(x, y, b; g^y, g^b), \ldots, \partial_{y_M} \vec{D}_O(x, y, b; g^y, g^b))}{\nabla_y \vec{D}_O(x, y, b; g^y, g^b) y},$$

$$(r_1, \ldots, r_J) = C \frac{(\partial_{b_1} \vec{D}_O(x, y, b; g^y, g^b), \ldots, \partial_{b_J} \vec{D}_O(x, y, b; g^y, g^b))}{\nabla_y \vec{D}_O(x, y, b; g^y, g^b) y},$$

where R is observed total revenue.

10.3 Empirical Application

10.3.1 *Data*

We use FDIC data for US banks for the period 2002–2016. We follow the intermediation approach (see Sealey and Lindley, 1977) to select the inputs and outputs of the banks' production technology. The inputs comprise labor measured by total employees (full-time equivalent), physical capital measured by bank premises and fixed assets, customer deposits, borrowed funds, Tier 1 (core) capital comprising common equity plus noncumulative perpetual preferred stock plus minority interests in consolidated subsidiaries less goodwill and other ineligible intangible assets. There are three desirable outputs, real estate loans, other loans and leases and total securities, and one undesirable output, provisions for loan and lease losses. We measure the price of labor as salaries and employee benefits over the total number of employees, and the price of physical capital as premises and equipment expenses over bank premises and fixed assets. The price of deposits is defined as the ratio of interest paid on deposits over total deposits, and the price of borrowed funds as interest expense on demand notes issued by the US treasury and other borrowed money over borrowed funds. The

Table 10.1: Descriptive Statistics — Bank Inputs and Outputs

	2002–2016	Mean	Std. dev.	Min	Max
Inputs–Outputs	Inputs				
	EMP	7.079	24.093	0.157	235.18
	K	0.357	1.085	0.02	11.56
	D	32.108	125.175	1.205	1480.24
	BF	3.977	13.961	0.05	212.69
	T1	3.648	13.962	0.012	179.34
	Desired Outputs				
	RELN	13.179	42.538	0.000	475.68
	OLN	12.635	48.342	0.001	575.18
	SEC	8.365	33.390	0.001	407.74
	Undesired Output				
	PLL	0.284	1.397	0.0001	29.39
	TA	46.375	178.723	2.001	2082.8
Size	Prices				
	PEMP	72.506	25.154	20.176	198.12
	PK	0.2926	0.1227	0.003	0.5986
	PD	0.0135	0.0106	0.0001	0.099
	PBF	0.0309	0.0218	0.0001	0.0999
	PL	0.0542	0.0172	0.0002	0.2617
	PSEC	0.0375	0.0211	0.0003	0.3478

Notes: EMP is number of employees measured in thousands, K is fixed assets, D is deposits, BF is borrowed funds, T1 is Tier 1 (core) capital, RELN is real estate loans, OLN is other loans, SEC is total securities, TA is total assets, PPL is provisions for loan and lease losses, all measured in billions of US dollars. PEMP is price of labor in thousands of US dollars, PK is the price of physical capital, PD is price of deposits, PBF is price of other borrowed funds, PLN is price of loans and PSEC is price of securities.

price of loans is measured as interest income on loans over total loans, and the price of securities as securities gains (losses) plus interest income on securities over total securities. Note that we do not have separate data on interest income from real estate loans and other loans and leases.

Table 10.1 presents the descriptive statistics of the data for the entire period (2002–2016). As expected, the input and output data are highly (right) skewed. Total assets are also highly right skewed (median 6.78 billion). The cost of borrowed funds is much higher on average than the cost of deposits, whereas loans appear to be more profitable than other earning assets.

10.3.2 *Empirical results*

We estimate DDFs by setting the values of the directional vector equal to unity. More specifically, we set $g^x = \bar{1}, g^y = \bar{1}, g^b = \bar{1}$ for the non-oriented DDF. Since equity capital is a quasi-fixed input, we set its associated value

Table 10.2: Descriptive Statistics — Bank Performance Indicators

	Mean	Std. dev.	Min	Max
		2002–2006		
DDF	0.958	0.066	0.443	1
CCAP (%)	8.140	2.745	4.745	43.606
ROA (%)	1.260	0.833	−4.579	11.667
		2007–2010		
DDF	0.967	0.056	0.426	1
CCAP (%)	8.567	2.491	0.399	28.159
ROA (%)	0.103	1.949	−18.169	8.104
		2011–2016		
DDF	0.981	0.044	0.530	1
CCAP (%)	9.805	1.896	2.230	27.945
ROA (%)	0.962	0.835	−12.084	9.159

Notes: DDF is the efficiency scores based an input DDF, output DDF and non-oriented distance function, respectively. For convenience, efficiency scores are reported in the range of zero to one, by rescaling the distance function values as $1/(1 + D_T)$. CCAP is core capital (leverage) ratio. ROA is return on assets.

in the direction vector equal to zero. Table 10.2 reports average efficiency scores based on different specifications of the distance function across the three sample periods. A bank that produces on the frontier is efficient and the DDF takes on a value of zero, with values greater than zero indicating inefficiency for the given g-directional vector. For ease of exposition, the DDF efficiency scores are reported in Table 10.2 in the range of zero to one, by rescaling the distance function values as $1/(1 + D_T)$. Bank efficiency is highest in the post-crisis period, and this finding is consistent across the three different efficiency measures. As expected, efficiency scores from the non-oriented DDF are greater (and less variable) than their counterparts obtained from the partial orientation models (DDF_I and DDF_O), since DDF allows banks to adjust both inputs and outputs simultaneously. Table 10.2 also shows that consistent with stricter regulatory requirements, the bank capitalization ratio (CCAP) is highest in the post-crisis period. As expected, return on assets (ROA) is lowest during the financial crisis period. Figure 10.1 presents time plots of the average shadow price of equity capital, the price of deposits and the price of other borrowed funds. The results are rather striking as they demonstrate a very high shadow cost of bank equity capital during the period leading to the subprime and global financial crisis at levels far in excess of what was deemed at the time to be an appropriate price of capital commensurate with perceived levels of market

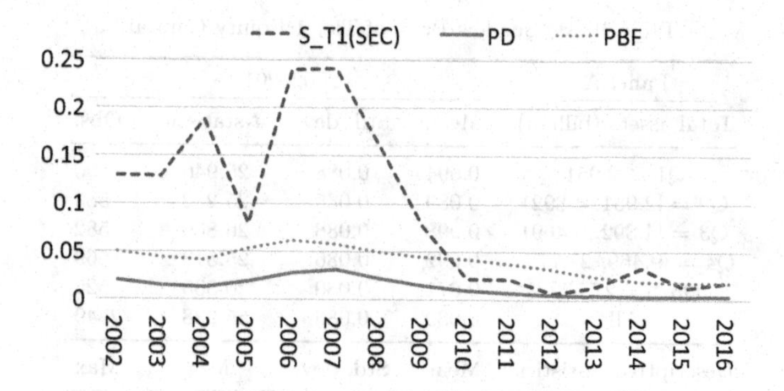

Fig. 10.1: Shadow Price of Tier1 Capital (Annual Averages)

Notes: S_T1(SEC) is the shadow price of Tier 1 capital when the price of Securities is known, PD is the price of deposits and PBF is the price of other borrowed funds.

risk. As to be expected, the price of debt is below the price of equity, albeit our estimates indicate that the price of equity is trending below the price of borrowed funds in the post-crisis period, in part reflecting the process of deleveraging by banks in response to stricter capital requirements but also due to increased risk aversion. Table 10.3 provides further information on the shadow price of capital, specifically it shows how the cost of equity varies across different bank size quantiles. Panel A shows that larger banks on average face, as expected, a lower cost of equity. Panel B shows the average cost of equity across the three sample subperiods: before, during and after the crisis. There is a sizable drop in the cost of equity in the post-crisis period commensurate with extensive bank deleveraging. Figure 10.2 presents time plots of the actual price of total loans, the shadow prices of real estate loans, other loans and leases and provisions for loans and leases constructed using information on the actual price of securities. We observe high shadow prices prior to and during the subprime crisis reflecting the riskiness of bank loan portfolios at the time. The shadow price for provisions for loan losses tracks much lower than loan prices suggesting provision estimates may have kept the opportunity cost of loan losses artificially low. A different explanation may be that the low shadow price for loan losses is commensurate with high shadow prices of loans, meaning that if loans were priced correctly to reflect their riskiness the opportunity cost for loan losses would have been low.

We turn next to investigate the association between the shadow price of equity capital and bank characteristics. Table 10.4 presents panel regression

Table 10.3: Shadow Price of Tier 1 Equity Capital

Panel A	2002–2016			
Total assets (billion)	Mean	Std. dev.	t-statistic	Obs.
Q1 < 2.951	0.094	0.088	25.946	590
Q2 = [2.951, 4.892)	0.089	0.085	25.282	583
Q3 = [4.892, 9.469)	0.098	0.088	26.866	582
Q4 = [9.469, 27.772)	0.092	0.086	25.518	569
Q5 >= 27.772	0.071	0.080	20.335	525
All	0.089	0.086	55.238	2849
Descriptive statistics	**Mean**	**Std. dev.**	**Min**	**Max**
		2002–2006		
S_T1(SEC)	0.149	0.071	0.001	0.299
		2007–2010		
S_T1(SEC)	0.120	0.09	0.001	0.299
		2011–2016		
S_T1(SEC)	0.017	0.015	0.001	0.221

Notes: S_T1(SE) indicates the shadow price for Tier 1 capital (T1) calculated from a non-oriented DDF using a cross-over pricing rule with known price of securities.

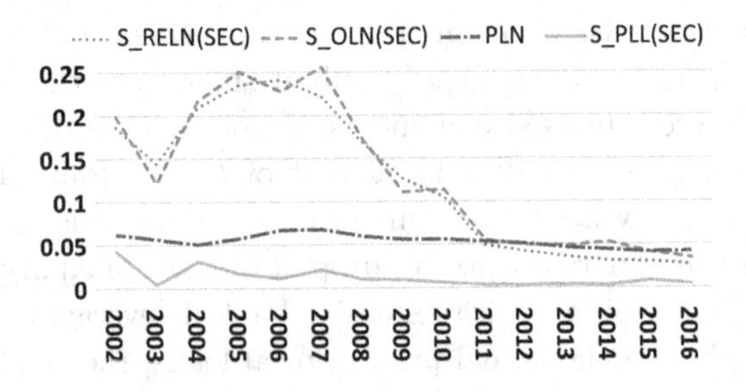

Fig. 10.2: Prices of Loans and Leases (Annual Averages)
Notes: S_RELN(SEC) is the shadow price of Real Estate Loans, S_OLN(SEC) is the shadow price of Other Loans, S_PLL(SEC) is the shadow price of provisions for loan losses when the price of Securities is known and PLN is the Price of loans.

results with cross-section and period fixed effects. We find that better capitalized banks face on average lower capital costs. Similarly, banks with more diversified revenue sources, specifically those with higher non-interest income to total assets and total securities to total assets, also face lower capital costs. On the other hand, banks with larger shares of real estate loans in their loan portfolio face higher capital costs. The effect of size

Table 10.4: Shadow Price of Capital Panel Regression (2002–2016)

	Estimate (t-ratio)	Estimate (t-ratio)	Estimate (t-ratio)	Estimate (t-ratio)
Constant	0.106 (25.937)	0.104 (24.989)	0.113 (23.303)	0.094 (10.762)
CCR	−0.186 (−4.104)	−0.141 (−2.932)	−0.151 (−3.126)	−0.147 (−3.055)
NII_TA		−0.136 (−2.642)	−0.146 (−2.850)	−0.145 (−2.824)
SEC_TA			−0.042 (−3.678)	−0.040 (−3.531)
RELN_LOANS				0.027 (2.642)
R^2-adj		0.869	0.869	0.869
DW		1.770	1.756	1.761

Notes: Panel regression with cross-section and period fixed effects. The dependent variable is the shadow price of equity capital. CCR is core capital ratio, NII_TA is non-interest income to total assets ratio, SEC_TA is the securities to total assets ratio, RELN_LN is real estate loans to total loans ratio.

measured by (log) total assets or number of full-time employees was not significant in the shadow price regressions.

10.4 Conclusion

In this chapter, we have applied the pricing rules developed in earlier parts of the book to estimate the shadow price of bank equity capital and non-performing loans for US banks during the period 2002–2016. One advantage of our approach is that we have been able to price equity for both listed and non-listed banks since we require no information on the market price of the bank. We have obtained some interesting results highlighting the risks of overambitious balance sheet expansions. Our estimates indicate excessive levels of shadow prices for equity capital stemming from highly leveraged bank positions conducive to excessive risk-taking. These findings are very informative since they provide quantitative assessment of the wedge that presumably existed between the shadow price and market price of risk during the period leading up to the subprime crisis. Panel regression results confirm the negative relation between core capital and its shadow price. Similarly, we find less diversified banks and banks with a larger share of real estate loans in their portfolio face higher equity capital costs.

Chapter 11

Network Production and Shadow Prices of Knowledge Outputs

William L. Weber

11.1 Introduction

Knowledge production is an important driver of productivity growth. However, since knowledge tends to be non-rival and non-exclusive, it might be under-produced by private firms if they find it difficult to capture its spillover effects. Governments support knowledge production by directly funding research and development, by supporting human capital development through higher education, by supporting intellectual property rights such as patents and by offering tax incentives to private firms that undertake research and development projects. In 2010–2011, the US federal government financed over half the spending on basic research while the private sector contributed less than one fourth (*Economic Report of the President*). Adams (1990) estimated that approximately 0.5% of US productivity growth during 1953–1990 was due to academic research. Recent work by Elnasri and Fox (2017) estimated that a 1% increase in higher education research spending increased Australian productivity growth by 0.4% during 1993–1994 to 2012–2013.

Nanoscience, engineering and technology are emerging fields that study the restructuring of matter at the atomic and molecular level. Such restructuring creates materials with new properties and functions. In medicine, nanotechnology helps deliver drugs that target cancer cells with fewer adverse side effects (Case, 2011). Nanotechnology is also expected to help slow carbon emissions as it finds uses in solar power, lithium batteries and artificial photosynthesis that grows 'green' fuels. In 2003, Congress passed the 21st Century Nanotechnology R&D Act which authorized funding for five agencies: National Science Foundation, Department of Energy, NASA, National Institute of Standards and Technology, and the Environmental Protection Agency (Roco, 2016). Funding for nanoscience and technology grew from approximately $400 million in 2000 to $1.5 billion in 2005. After peaking at $2.5 billion in 2009, federal funding for nanotechnology R&D fell back to $1.5 billion in the 2016 federal budget.[1]

This chapter examines the production of nanobiotechnology knowledge outputs at 29 universities from 1993 to 2005. University departments in life sciences, physical sciences and engineering have research budgets from which they fund researchers, laboratories and equipment. In turn, the researchers and their capital work to produce patents, Ph.D. graduates and publications related to nanobiotechnology. Publications are an intermediate output that expands future production possibilities in two ways: first, by enhancing the university's own production of knowledge outputs and second, by spilling over to add to the knowledge base of other universities. The network model derives prices for the knowledge outputs based on their estimated tradeoffs given the research budget.

11.2 Knowledge Production Spillovers

From 1947 to 1973 multi-factor productivity growth averaged 1.87% per year but then slowed to 0.4% per year from 1973 to 1980.[2] To promote technology transfer from the public sector to the private sector and thereby foster productivity growth, the Bayh–Dole Act of 1980 allowed universities to patent and license research that had been funded by the federal government (Weber and Xia, 2011). The Act caused some researchers to worry that universities would expand the production of applied research at the expense of basic research — the public good of knowledge widely disseminated. An equity argument can also be made against the Bayh–Dole Act if diseases afflicting poor people in developing countries are neglected

[1] These are constant 2015 dollars.

[2] Federal Reserve Economic Data Series MFPNFBS: Private Non-Farm Business Sector: Multi-factor productivity. Multi-factor productivity is measured by a Tornquist output index with inputs of labor and capital.

by private licensees of a university's patent, such as pharmaceutical firms (de Campos, 2015).

Determining the extent to which basic research and applied research are substitutes or complements can impact the debate about the loss of public good associated with Bayh–Dole. Azoulay, Ding and Stuart (2009), Fabrizio and Di Minin (2008), Foltz, Kim and Barham (2003), and Foltz, Barham and Kim (2007) found evidence that basic research and patenting activity are complementary. In contrast, Weber and Xia (2011) estimated Morishima output elasticities of transformation and found that for nanobiotechnology research, university patents are dual complements with publications and Ph.D. students. Thus, university nanobiotechnology patents can only be supported by a decline in the relative values of publications and Ph.D. students.

Fukuyama, Weber and Xia (2015) built a network DEA model of knowledge production where universities produce final outputs of nanobiotechnology patents and Ph.D. students and an intermediate product — publications — which generates spillover effects. A university's own publications adds to its own knowledge stock and also enhances the knowledge stock at other universities as their scientists and engineers read and incorporate others' publications into their own research.

11.3 Theory and Method

Knowledge embedded in a university's publications is an intermediate product and can be represented by a network production model. In this framework research publications produced in one period become an input to expand production possibilities in a subsequent period in two ways. First, publications enhance the university's own human capital base and thereby expand the university's own production technology. Second, researchers at other universities can draw on those publications and use them to augment their own production possibilities.[3]

The network production model developed here draws on the work of Färe and Grosskopf (1996), Kao (2013, 2014), Färe, Grosskopf and Weber (2016) and Fukuyama, Weber and Xia (2015).

[3]Some literature (see de Campos, 2015) suggests that university patenting activity delays publications and the dissemination of knowledge.

11.3.1 *Network technology and directional output distance function*

Production takes place in $t = 1, \ldots, T$ periods by $k = 1, \ldots, K$ universities. Final outputs produced by the jth university are $fy_j^t = (fy_{j1}^t, \ldots, fy_{jM}^t)$. Each university also produces a single intermediate product, iy_{j1}^t. This intermediate product enhances university $j's$ own production in the subsequent period and also spills over to other universities. In period t the spillover input that producer j receives from other universities is $iy_{j2}^{t-1} = \sum_{k \neq j}^{K} iy_{k1}^{t-1}$. Let the two intermediate products from period $t-1$ — the university's own intermediate product and the spillover product from other universities — be represented by the vector $iy_j^{t-1} = (iy_{j1}^{t-1}, iy_{j2}^{t-1})$. Producers also have a budget, c_j^t, which they use to purchase inputs. Dropping the j subscript the production technology at t is represented by the set

$$P^t(iy^{t-1}, c^t) = \{(fy^t, iy_1^t) : \ (iy^{t-1}, c^t) \text{ can produce } (fy^t, iy_1^t)\}. \quad (11.1)$$

Figure 11.1 depicts the network technology. In period t the DMU (decision-making unit) has a budget c^t with which to hire inputs and it has access to the intermediate product it produced in the previous period, iy_1^{t-1}. In addition, DMU j has access to the sum of the intermediate product produced by all other DMUs: $iy_{j2}^{t-1} = \sum_{k \neq j}^{K} iy_{k1}^{t-1}$. To further illustrate the spillover effect assume that there are three DMUs which, in $t-1$,

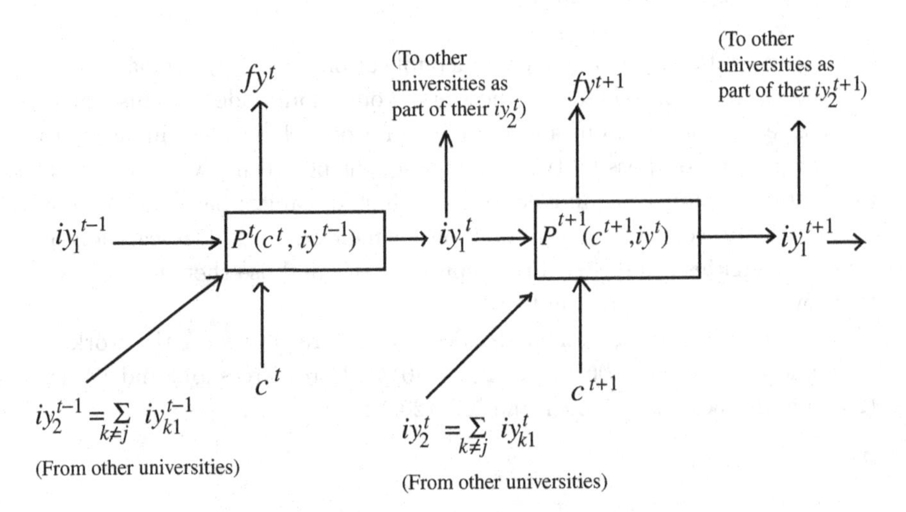

Fig. 11.1: Network Production with Spillovers

produce $iy_{11}^{t-1} = 5$, $iy_{21}^{t-1} = 7$ and $iy_{31}^{t-1} = 8$. In period t, the spillovers received by the three DMUs are $iy_{12}^{t-1} = 7 + 8 = 15$, $iy_{22}^{t-1} = 5 + 8 = 13$ and $iy_{32}^{t-1} = 5 + 7 = 12$. Figure 11.1 shows that in period t, DMU j uses c_j^t, iy_{j1}^{t-1} and iy_{j2}^{t-1} to produce final outputs (fy^t) and the intermediate product (iy_1^t).

The network technology depicted in Figure 11.1 is represented by a directional output distance function in cost space. This distance function seeks the maximum simultaneous expansion in all outputs for a given directional vector and budget used to hire inputs. Let $g = (g_1, \ldots, g_M, g_{M+1})$ be a directional vector (path) along which the M final outputs and the single intermediate product are expanded. To ease the notation let $y^t = (fy_1^t, \ldots, fy_M^t, iy_1^t)$ represent the vector of final outputs and the single intermediate product. The directional output distance function takes the form

$$\vec{D}_o^t(y^t, iy^{t-1}, c^t; g) = \max\{\beta : y^t + \beta g) \in P^t(iy^{t-1}, c^t)\}. \tag{11.2}$$

The directional distance function inherits its properties from the production technology. These properties are

$$\begin{aligned}
&\text{(i)}\ \ \vec{D}_o^t(y^t, iy^{t-1}, c^t; g) \geq 0 \Leftrightarrow y^t \in P^t(iy^{t-1}, c^t) \\
&\text{(ii)}\ \ \vec{D}_o^t(y^t, iy^{t-1}, c^t; g) \geq \vec{D}_o^t(\overline{y}^t, iy^{t-1}, c^t; g) \quad \text{for } y^t \leq \overline{y}^t \\
&\text{(iii)}\ \ \vec{D}_o^t(y^t, iy^{t-1}, c^t; g) \leq \vec{D}_o^t(y^t, \overline{iy}^{t-1}, c^t; g) \quad \text{for } iy^{t-1} \leq \overline{iy}^{t-1} \\
&\text{(iv)}\ \ \vec{D}_o^t(y^t, iy^{t-1}, c^t; g) \leq \vec{D}_o^t(y^t, iy^{t-1}, \overline{c}^t; g) \quad \text{for } c^t \leq \overline{c}^t.
\end{aligned} \tag{11.3}$$

The properties are: (i) feasibility; (ii) $\vec{D}_o^t(\cdot)$ is non-increasing in y; and (iii) and (iv) mean that $\vec{D}_o^t(\cdot)$ is non-decreasing in iy^{t-1} and c^t, respectively.

By definition, the distance function acquires the translation property:

$$\vec{D}_o^t(y^t + \alpha g, iy^{t-1}, c^t; g) = \vec{D}_o^t(y^t, iy^{t-1}, c^t; g) - \alpha, \tag{11.4}$$

which is the additive counterpart to homogeneity of the Shephard distance function.

The directional output distance function measures technical inefficiency. Efficient producers have $\vec{D}_o^t(y^t, iy^{t-1}, c^t; g) = 0$, meaning that it is not possible to expand outputs given the budget and intermediate outputs from the previous period. Inefficient producers have $\vec{D}_o^t(y^t, iy^t, iy^{t-1}, c^t; g) > 0$, with higher values indicating greater inefficiency in the g direction. The directional vector, g, determines the path along which outputs are projected to the frontier. When $g = (1, \ldots, 1)$ the directional output distance function gives the maximum feasible unit expansion in all outputs.

When $g = (fy_1, \ldots, fy_M, iy_1)$ the directional output distance function gives the maximum feasible proportional expansion in all outputs. One might also constrain some proper subset of the directional vector to be zero, so that expansions in some outputs are measured holding other outputs constant.

11.3.2 *Shadow prices*

We use the directional output distance function to estimate shadow prices for the final outputs and the intermediate product. Here we extend the work of Färe, Grosskopf and Weber (2016) to obtain those shadow prices. The revenue function is dual to the directional output distance function. Let the price vector of the M final outputs and the single intermediate product be represented by $p^t = (p_1^t, \ldots, p_M^t, p_{M+1}^t)$. The revenue function is written as

$$R(c^t, iy^{t-1}, p^t) = \max_y \left\{ p^t y : \ \vec{D}_o^t(y^t, iy^{t-1}, c^t; g) \geq 0 \right\}, \tag{11.5}$$

where $p^t y^t = \sum_{m=1}^{M} p_m^t f y_m^t + p_{M+1}^t iy^t$ is revenue from final outputs plus revenue from the intermediate product. When the production technology, $P^t(iy^{t-1}, c^t)$, is convex, the duality can be written as

$$c^t = p^t y^t = R(c^t, iy^{t-1}, p^t) - \vec{D}_o^t(y^t, iy^{t-1}, c^t; g)pg. \tag{11.6}$$

In words, actual revenues, $p^t y^t$, equal the difference between maximal revenues, $R(c^t, iy^{t-1}, p^t)$, and the value of the lost output due to technical inefficiency, $\vec{D}_o^t(y^t, iy^{t-1}, c^t; g)p^t g$. To derive the shadow prices we first differentiate (11.6) with respect to outputs:

$$p^t = (p_1^t, \ldots, p_M^t, p_{M+1}^t) = \ -\nabla_y \ \vec{D}_o^t(y^t, iy^{t-1}, c^t; g)p^t g. \tag{11.7}$$

Next, multiply (11.7) (y^t) to get

$$p^t y^t = \ -\nabla_y \ \vec{D}_o^t(y^t, iy^{t-1}, c^t; g)p^t g y^t \tag{11.8}$$

and then solve (11.8) for $p^t g$

$$p^t g = \ -\frac{p^t y^t}{\nabla_y \vec{D}_o^t(y^t, iy^{t-1}, c^t; g)y^t}. \tag{11.9}$$

Finally, recognizing that $p^t y^t = c^t$ from (11.6), substitute (11.9) into (11.7) to obtain the pricing vector

$$p^t = \ c^t \frac{\nabla_y \vec{D}_o^t(y^t, iy^{t-1}, c^t; g)}{\nabla_y \vec{D}_o^t(y^t, iy^{t-1}, c^t; g)y^t}. \tag{11.10}$$

Some shadow pricing methods use Shephard or directional distance functions to recover the marginal rate of transformation between outputs and then exploit the first-order conditions for revenue maximization. Those conditions require the marginal rate of transformation to equal the ratio of prices. Given one known market price, the prices of other non-market goods and services can be recovered (see Färe *et al.*, 2005). The pricing formula (11.10) offers an alternative to those shadow pricing methods in that it does not require an observed market price. Instead, (11.10) only requires data on outputs produced, intermediate products from the previous period and the budget.

11.4 The Quadratic Functional Form

Chambers (1998) suggests using a quadratic functional form to estimate the directional distance function given in (11.2). The quadratic form allows restrictions to be placed on the coefficients consistent with the translation property. In a Monte Carlo simulation Färe, Martins-Filho and Vardanyan (2010) found that the quadratic directional distance function outperformed a translog (radial) output distance function. Furthermore, unlike a translog functional form, the quadratic form allows the outputs and intermediate products to take values of zero. This feature is quite useful since several of the universities in our sample produce zero output in some periods.

We assume that production takes place in $t = 1\ldots,T$ periods by $k = 1,\ldots,K$ producers. Let $iy_k^{t-1} = (iy_{k1}^{t-1}, iy_{k2}^{t-1})$ represent the vector of intermediate products generated in period $t-1$. These intermediate products are the university's own intermediate product iy_{k1}^{t-1} and the intermediate product that spills over from other universities, iy_{k2}^{t-1}. Producers use the intermediate products generated from the previous period and their current budget, c_k^t, to hire other inputs. Final outputs and the single intermediate product are represented by the $1 \times (M+1)$ vector $y_k^t = (fy_{k1}^t, \ldots, fy_{kM}^t, iy_{k1}^t)$.

The quadratic directional output distance function takes the form

$$\begin{aligned}\vec{D}_o^t(y_k^t, iy_k^{t-1}, c_k^t; g) = {} & \alpha_0 + \sum_{m=1}^{M+1} \alpha_m y_{km}^t + \frac{1}{2}\sum_{m=1}^{M+1}\sum_{m'=1}^{M+1} \alpha_{mm'} y_{km}^t y_{km'}^t \\ & + \sum_{j=1}^{2} \beta_j iy_{kj}^{t-1} + \frac{1}{2}\sum_{j=1}^{2}\sum_{j'=1}^{2} \beta_{jj'} iy_{kj}^{t-1} iy_{kj'}^{t-1}\end{aligned}$$

$$+ \delta_1 c_k^t + \frac{1}{2}\delta_2 c_k^t c_k^t + \sum_{m=1}^{M+1} \theta_m y_{km}^t c_k^t + \sum_{j=1}^{2} \gamma_j iy_j^{t-1} c_k^t$$

$$+ \sum_{m=1}^{M+1}\sum_{j=1}^{2} \phi_{mj} y_{km}^t iy_{kj}^{t-1}. \tag{11.11}$$

The directional vector g is not parameterized in (11.11). Instead, the translation property imposes restrictions on the coefficients for a given directional vector (Hudgins and Primont, 2007). The translation restrictions are

$$\sum_{m=1}^{M+1} \alpha_m g_m = -1, \ \sum_{m=1}^{M+1} \alpha_{mm'} g_m = 0, \quad m' = 1, \ldots, M+1$$

$$\sum_{m=1}^{M+1} \theta_m g_m = 0, \ \sum_{m=1}^{M+1} \phi_{mj} g_m = 0, \quad j = 1, \ldots, J. \tag{11.12}$$

To estimate (11.11) we use the deterministic method of Aigner and Chu (1968). This method chooses the parameters α_0, α_m, $\alpha_{mm'}$, β_j, $\beta_{jj'}$, δ_1, δ_2, θ_m, γ_j and ϕ_{mj} to minimize the distance from the observed outputs to the frontier of $P^t(iy^{t-1}, c^t)$. The minimization also imposes the feasibility and monotonicity conditions as well as symmetry of the second-order coefficients and the translation property. This deterministic problem is

$$\min \sum_{t=1}^{T}\sum_{k=1}^{K} \vec{D}_o^t(y_k^t, iy_k^{t-1}, c_k^t; g)$$

s.t.

$$\text{(i)} \ \vec{D}_o^t(y_k^t, iy_k^{t-1}, c_k^t; g) \geq 0, \ k = 1, \ldots, K, \ t = 1, \ldots, T$$

$$\text{(ii)} \ \alpha_{mm'} = \alpha_{m'm}, \ m \neq m', \ \beta_{jj'} = \beta_{j'j}, \ j \neq j'$$

$$\text{(iii)} \ \sum_{m=1}^{M+1} \alpha_m g_m = -1, \ \sum_{m=1}^{M+1} \alpha_{mm'} g_m = 0, \ m' = 1, \ldots, M+1,$$

$$\sum_{m=1}^{M+1} \theta_m g_m = 0, \ \sum_{m=1}^{M+1} \phi_{mj} g_m = 0, \ j = 1, \ldots, J$$

$$\text{(iv)} \ \partial \vec{D}^t(\cdot)/\partial y_{km}^t \leq 0, \ m = 1, \ldots, M+1, \ k = 1, \ldots, K, \ t = 1, \ldots, T$$

$$\text{(v)} \ \partial \vec{D}^t(\cdot)/\partial iy_{kj}^{t-1} \geq 0, \ j = 1, \ 2, \ k = 1, \ldots, K, \ t = 1, \ldots, T$$

$$\text{(vi)} \ \partial \vec{D}^t(\cdot)/\partial c_k^t \geq 0, \ k = 1, \ldots, K, \ t = 1, \ldots, T. \tag{11.13}$$

The restrictions in (11.13) impose feasibility (i), symmetry of the cross-product terms (ii), the translation property (iii), and ensure that the directional distance function is non-increasing in y^t (iv), is non-decreasing in intermediate products iy^{t-1} (v) and is non-decreasing in the budget c^t (vi).

Once (11.13) is estimated the shadow pricing formula (11.10) can be used. For the quadratic directional distance function the shadow prices for the M final outputs and the single intermediate product are

$$p_{km}^t = \frac{(\alpha_m + \sum_{m=1}^{M+1} \alpha_{mm'} y_{km'}^t + \theta_m c_k^t + \sum_{j=1}^{2} \phi_{mj} iy_{kj}^{t-1}) c_k^t}{\sum_{m=1}^{M+1} (\alpha_m + \sum_{m=1}^{M+1} \alpha_{mm'} y_{km'}^t + \theta_m c_k^t + \sum_{j=1}^{2} \phi_{mj} iy_{kj}^{t-1}) y_m^t},$$

$$m = 1, \ldots, M+1, \quad k = 1, \ldots, K, \quad t = 1, \ldots, T. \tag{11.14}$$

11.5 Data and Estimates

The data are from 1990 to 2005 on 29 universities that engaged in nanobiotechnology research. The knowledge outputs are patents, Ph.D. graduates and publications.[4] It typically takes multiple periods to produce a publication, a patent, or a Ph.D. student. I follow Weber and Xia (2011) and Fukuyama, Weber and Xia (2015) and take a 3 year moving average of patents (y_1), Ph.D. students (y_2) and publications (iy_1). The budget equals the 3 year moving average of the sum of real research expenditures in life sciences, physical sciences, engineering and NSF grants. Given the 3 year moving average of outputs and budget and the lagged value of intermediate products, iy^{t-1}, there are data for 13 years (1993–2005) and 29 universities to estimate the model (11.13).

Table 11.1 reports descriptive statistics for the pooled sample of 377 observations. Figure 11.2 graphs the trends in the average outputs and the budget during 1993–2005 with the averages normalized to 1 in 1993. Significant growth in outputs occurs during the period as patents increased by a factor of 5.1, Ph.D. students increased by a factor of 8.5 and publications increased by a factor of 7.5 from their 1993 levels. In contrast, the budget increased by only 1.43 times from 1993 to 2005. The average annual number

[4]The universities are Case Western, Columbia, Washington University, Cornell, Georgia Tech, Harvard, Johns Hopkins, Kansas State, North Carolina State, Northwestern, Ohio State, Pennsylvania State, Rice, Stanford, Tufts, UCLA, Cincinnati, Illinois, Kansas, Maryland, Michigan, Missouri, New Mexico, Pennsylvania, Texas, Utah, Virginia, Washington and Wisconsin.

Table 11.1: Descriptive Statistics

Variable	Description	Mean	Std. dev.	Min.	Max
fy_1	Patents	3.38	3.79	0.00	25.00
fy_2	Ph.D. grads.	1.38	1.60	0.00	11.00
iy_1	Own publications	6.21	6.62	0.00	45.33
iy_1^{-1}	Lagged own publications	4.97	4.98	0.00	33.33
iy_2^{-1}	Lagged spillover publications	139.11	87.46	41.33	365.33
c	Budget (millions of 2005 dollars)	341.35	211.62	27.15	1263.15

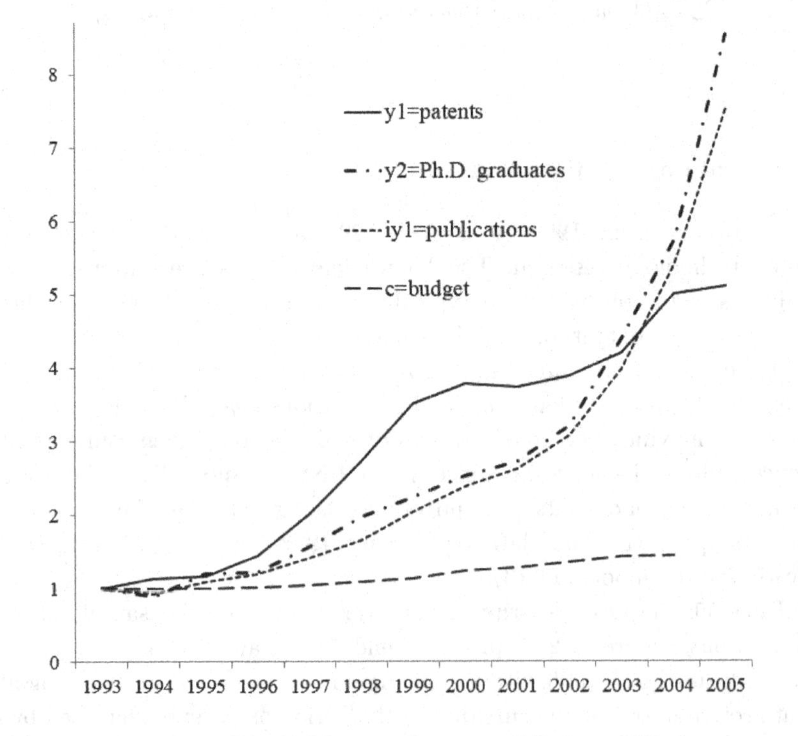

Fig. 11.2: Trend of Average Outputs and Budget, 1993=1

of patents surpassed its pooled mean of 3.38 in 1999. The average annual number of Ph.D. graduates in nanobiotechnology surpassed its pooled mean of 1.38 in 2002, and the average annual number of publications surpassed its pooled mean of 6.21 in 2001. The budget is deflated by the GDP deflator with a base year of 2005. The average annual real budget surpassed its pooled mean of 341 million dollars in 2000.

Table 11.2: Estimates

Coefficient	Variable	Estimate
α_0	constant	−0.09660
α_1	y_1^t	−0.08671
α_2	y_2^t	−0.74008
α_3	y_3^t	−0.17321
α_{11}	$y_1^t y_1^t$	0.00566
α_{12}	$y_1^t y_2^t$	0.00334
α_{13}	$y_1^t y_3^t$	−0.00900
α_{22}	$y_2^t y_2^t$	−0.01341
α_{23}	$y_2^t y_3^t$	0.01007
α_{33}	y_3^2	−0.00107
β_1	iy_1^{t-1}	0.34927
β_2	iy_2^{t-1}	0.00686
β_{11}	$iy_1^{t-1} iy_1^{t-1}$	−0.02375
β_{12}	$iy_1^{t-1} iy_2^{t-1}$	0.00181
β_{22}	$iy_2^{t-1} iy_2^{t-1}$	−0.00004
δ_1	c^t	0.00245
δ_2	$c^t c^t$	0.00000
θ_1	$y_1^t c^t$	0.00013
θ_2	$y_2^t c^t$	−0.00001
θ_3	$y_3^t c^t$	−0.00012
γ_1	$iy_1^{t-1} c^t$	−0.00001
γ_2	$iy_2^{t-1} c^t$	0.00001
ϕ_{11}	$y_1^t iy_1^{t-1}$	−0.00216
ϕ_{12}	$y_1^t iy_2^{t-1}$	−0.00088
ϕ_{21}	$y_2^t iy_1^{t-1}$	0.00579
ϕ_{22}	$y_2^t iy_2^{t-1}$	0.00033
ϕ_{31}	$y_3^t iy_1^{t-1}$	0.00363
ϕ_{32}	$y_3^t iy_2^{t-1}$	0.00055

The directional vector, $g = (1, 1, 1)$, is used to estimate the directional distance function using the deterministic method (11.13). This choice means that $\vec{D}_o^t(y^t, iy^t, iy^{t-1}, c^t; 1)$ equals the simultaneous loss in the two final outputs and the intermediate product because of inefficiency or, alternatively, the potential gain in outputs if the university were to become efficient. Table 11.2 reports the parameter estimates. The parameter estimates and the actual outputs and budget are used to implement the pricing formula.

Table 11.3 reports the estimates of $\vec{D}_o^t(y^t, iy^t, iy^{t-1}, c^t; 1)$, the number of frontier universities and the output prices by year. The frontier universities are Cornell, Rice and Utah in 2003; Texas in 1996; Harvard, Penn State and Rice in 1998; Johns Hopkins and Penn State in 1999; Michigan and the University of Washington in 2004; and Illinois in 2005. Inefficiency is

Table 11.3: Estimates of Inefficiency and Shadow Prices of Knowledge Outputs

	$\vec{D}_o^t(\cdot;1)$	DMUs on Frontier	Prices[a] of knowledge outputs: Patents(p_1)	Ph.D. grads(p_2)	Publications(p_3)
1993	0.555	3	48.28	425.03	124.19
1994	1.116	0	68.38	456.79	124.27
1995	0.789	0	57.66	373.62	99.66
1996	0.943	1	44.67	297.98	84.79
1997	0.807	0	34.76	205.94	58.96
1998	0.876	3	31.66	155.10	44.93
1999	0.939	2	28.97	119.92	35.95
2000	1.399	2	36.09	122.65	33.82
2001	1.859	0	35.98	105.33	28.58
2002	1.995	0	34.89	92.39	25.33
2003	2.092	0	36.95	80.52	20.78
2004	2.918	1	39.30	61.59	14.33
2005	5.214	0	78.25	88.36	8.13
All years	1.654	12	44.30	198.86	54.13

[a]Prices are in millions of constant 2005 dollars.

lowest in 1993 when the 29 universities on average could have produced an additional 0.55 patents, 0.55 Ph.D. students and 0.55 publications if they had produced on the frontier. Inefficiency goes up and down until 1997. From 1997 to 2005 inefficiency increases in every year, reaching a peak in 2005.

The prices of the three non-market outputs — patents (fy_1^t), Ph.D. graduates (fy_2^t) and publications (iy_1^t) — are reported in Table 11.3 and graphed in Figure 11.3. Ph.D. students had the highest average shadow price, \$199 million, and patents had the lowest average shadow price, \$44 million. The price of patents was highest in 2005, more than double its average price from 1997 to 2004. The price of publications, the intermediate product, fell from \$124 million in 1993 to \$8.13 million in 2005. The price of Ph.D. graduates also fell from \$457 million in 1994 to \$61 million in 2004.

Time substitution allows resources to be reallocated across periods so as to maximize total outputs or minimize costs or meet some other production objective (Färe *et al.*, 2012; Fukuyama, Weber and Xia, 2015). This intertemporal reallocation of resources can enhance production efficiency under certain conditions. First, if a producer operates in the range of increasing returns to scale then it is better to use resources intensively in a single period rather than spreading those resources over many periods. Likewise, when decreasing returns to scale exists, production efficiency can be enhanced by using resources less intensively over many periods. Second,

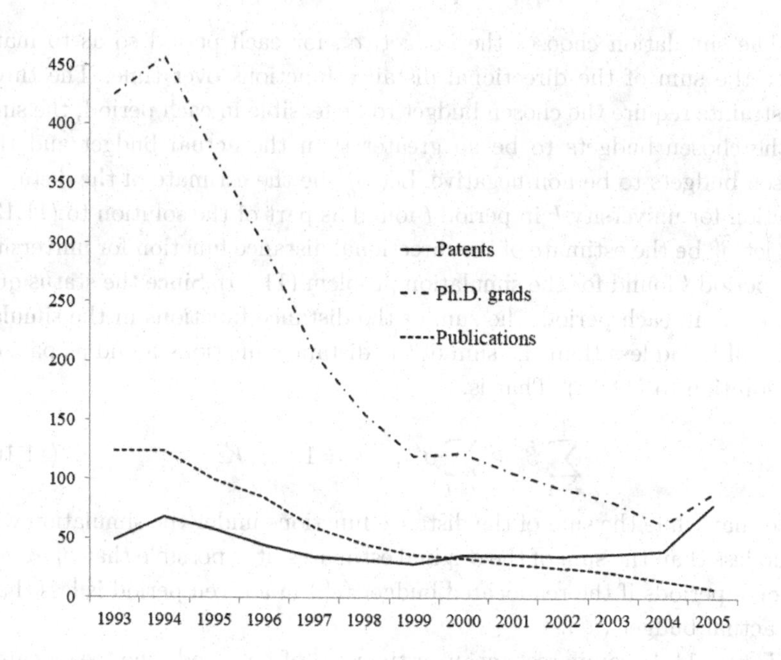

Fig. 11.3: Trend in Shadow Prices

when technological progress occurs it is better to delay production and use resources later so as to reap the benefits of progress. When technological regress occurs it is better to use the resources earlier in a period.

Here, we use time substitution to simulate changes in production when the university research budget is reallocated across periods. Let $C_k = \sum_{t=1}^{T} c_k^t$ equal total spending by university k over all the periods. The simulation reallocates total spending across all periods so as to maximize the sum of the distances of observed outputs to each period's frontier. The parameters from Table 11.2 are used in this simulation which is run $K = 29$ times, i.e., once for each of the 29 universities. The simulation finds the solution to the following problem:

$$\max_{c^t} \sum_{t=1}^{T} \vec{D}_o^t(y_k^t, iy_k^t, iy_k^{t-1}, c^t; g)$$

$$\text{s.t.} \quad \vec{D}_o^t(y_k^t, iy_k^t, iy_k^{t-1}, c^t; 1) \geq 0, \ t = 1, \ldots, T$$

$$\sum_{t=1}^{T} c^t \leq C_k$$

$$c_t \geq 0, \ t = 1, \ldots, T. \tag{11.15}$$

The simulation chooses the budget, c^t, for each period so as to maximize the sum of the directional distance functions over time. The three constraints require the chosen budget to be feasible in each period, the sum of the chosen budgets to be no greater than the actual budget and the chosen budgets to be non-negative. Let β_k^{*t} be the estimate of the distance function for university k in period t found as part of the solution to (11.13) and let $\tilde{\beta}_k^t$ be the estimate of the directional distance function for university k in period t found for the simulation problem (11.15). Since the status quo is feasible in each period, the sum of the distance functions in the simulation will be no less than the sum of the distance functions found as part of the solution to (11.13). That is,

$$\sum_{t=1}^{T} \tilde{\beta}_k^t \geq \sum_{t=1}^{T} \beta^{*t}, \quad k = 1, \ldots, K. \tag{11.16}$$

Note that while the sum of the distance functions under the simulation will be no less than the sum of the original estimates, it is possible that $\tilde{\beta}_k^t < \beta_k^{*t}$ in some periods if the reallocated budget ($\tilde{c}_k^t$) in a given period is less than the actual budget (c_k^t).

Table 11.4 compares mean estimates of $\tilde{\beta}^t$ and the reallocated budgets ($\tilde{c}_k^t$) under the simulation with the original estimates of β^t and actual budgets. The average actual budget (c^t) increases fairly smoothly throughout the period. In contrast, from 1993 to 1999, the optimal simulated budget is less than the actual budget. Then, from 2000 to 2005, average simulated budgets are greater than average actual budgets. Next, comparing $\tilde{\beta}^t$ with β^{*t}, we see a smaller distance to the simulated frontier than to the actual frontier from 1993 to 2000. The trend reverses during 2001 to 2005; there is a greater distance of observed outputs to the simulated frontier than from observed outputs to the actual frontier. This result is consistent with the monotonicity condition for the budget. The larger simulated budget granted in the later years increases the distance of observed outputs to the simulated frontier. Averaged over all years, the gains in patents, Ph.D. students and publications equals $(1.702 - 1.654) = 0.048$ per university per year. That is, the 29 universities could have produced about $1.4 = 0.048 \times 29$ additional patents, Ph.D. students and publications per year if they had been able to allocate their budgets in the manner suggested by the simulation.

Optimally reallocating the budget across the years also affects the prices of the three non-market knowledge outputs. The average simulated prices are reported in Table 11.5. The average price of the three knowledge outputs under the simulation are lower than the average shadow prices reported in

Table 11.4: Simulation Results

	Average inefficiency		Average budget	
	$\tilde{\beta}^t$	β^{*t}	$\tilde{c}^t$	c^t
1993	0.368	0.555	188.97	288.33
1994	0.950	1.116	218.65	288.23
1995	0.589	0.789	194.43	287.69
1996	0.777	0.943	216.51	288.92
1997	0.681	0.807	244.22	297.33
1998	0.771	0.876	284.55	313.31
1999	0.886	0.939	320.68	325.88
2000	1.392	1.399	364.72	352.97
2001	1.947	1.859	409.02	368.55
2002	2.089	1.995	420.41	390.14
2003	2.229	2.092	438.50	408.99
2004	3.339	2.918	520.58	413.99
2005	6.103	5.214	616.38	413.27
All years	1.702	1.654	341.35	341.35

Table 11.5: Prices of Knowledge Outputs Under the Simulated Budget

	Patents	Ph.D. grads	Publications
	$\tilde{p}_1$	$\tilde{p}_2$	$\tilde{p}_3$
1993	27.24	207.18	58.57
1994	35.94	244.65	70.01
1995	25.01	164.78	46.61
1996	27.20	187.46	55.27
1997	19.55	126.32	39.52
1998	16.18	106.54	38.30
1999	18.19	92.96	35.94
2000	27.57	105.62	36.31
2001	36.42	113.17	33.24
2002	36.54	102.42	29.27
2003	43.04	99.33	25.27
2004	59.16	108.81	25.35
2005	89.08	120.69	21.86
All years	36.16	136.92	39.66

Table 11.3. This difference occurs because of the reallocation of the budget from the earlier years, when only small quantities of the outputs are produced to the later years, when larger amounts of patents, Ph.D. graduates and publications are produced. The original shadow prices for patents and Ph.D. graduates (Table 11.3) are higher than the prices under the simulated reallocation of the budget until 2001, when the simulated prices

become greater than the original shadow prices. For publications, the original prices are greater than the simulated prices until 2000. As Table 11.4 shows, the simulated budget with reallocation is less than the actual budget until 2000.

11.6 On the Value of Knowledge Spillovers

Shadow prices of the three knowledge outputs — patents, Ph.D. graduates and the intermediate product of publications — have been derived using the parameter estimates of the quadratic directional distance function and the pricing formula in (11.14). Our final goal is to estimate the marginal external benefit of the intermediate product. Recall that the publications of university j in $t-1$ are an intermediate product that enhance production possibilities in t. In addition, university j gains access to the publications produced by other universities in the preceding period: $iy_{j2}^{t-1} = \sum_{k \neq j}^{t-1} iy_{k1}^{t-1}$. These spillover publications expand university j's production set $P^t(iy_j^{t-1}, c_j^t)$, where $iy_j^{t-1} = (iy_{j1}^{t-1}, iy_{j2}^{t-1})$.

To estimate the marginal external benefit we take the total differential of (11.11) and evaluate it for $dy_m^t = 0$, $i = 1, \ldots, M$ and $diy_1^t = 0$;

$$\frac{\partial \vec{D}^t(\cdot)}{\partial iy_2^t} diy_2^{t-1} + \frac{\partial \vec{D}^t(\cdot)}{\partial c^t} dc^t = 0. \tag{11.17}$$

The idea in (11.17) is that a one unit change in the spillover input, iy_2^{t-1}, would, because of the monotonicity conditions, require an offsetting change in the budget to keep the university on the same frontier. Rearranging (11.17) yields

$$\frac{dc^t}{diy_2^t} = -\frac{\partial \vec{D}^t(\cdot) \partial iy_2^{t-1}}{\partial \vec{D}^t(\cdot)/\partial c^t}. \tag{11.18}$$

Applying (11.18) for the quadratic form (11.11) the marginal external benefit received by each university is

$$\frac{dc_k^t}{diy_{k2}^t} = -\frac{\beta_2 + \sum_{j=1}^2 \beta_{j2} iy_{kj}^{t-1} + \gamma_2 c_k^t + \sum_{m=1}^{M+1} \phi_{m2} y_{km}^t}{\delta_1 + \delta_2 c_k^t + \sum_{m=1}^{M+1} \theta_m y_m^t + \sum_{j=1}^2 \gamma_j iy_j^{t-1}}, \quad k = 1, \ldots, K. \tag{11.19}$$

Table 11.6 reports the mean marginal external benefit by year, $-(dc^t/diy_2^{t-1})$. These estimates represent the increase in the budget that would be required for the average university to continue producing the same level of the three outputs if they did not receive the marginal publication from other universities. These values range from \$11.52 million in

Table 11.6: Mean MEB of Publications (in millions of)

Year	$-\frac{dc^t}{diy_2^{t-1}}$	Budget share
1993	11.52	0.033
1994	7.64	0.027
1995	8.47	0.030
1996	7.81	0.029
1997	7.81	0.028
1998	6.76	0.025
1999	6.39	0.022
2000	6.77	0.020
2001	7.45	0.019
2002	8.93	0.022
2003	11.42	0.026
2004	14.53	0.030
2005	21.37	0.041
All years	9.76	0.027

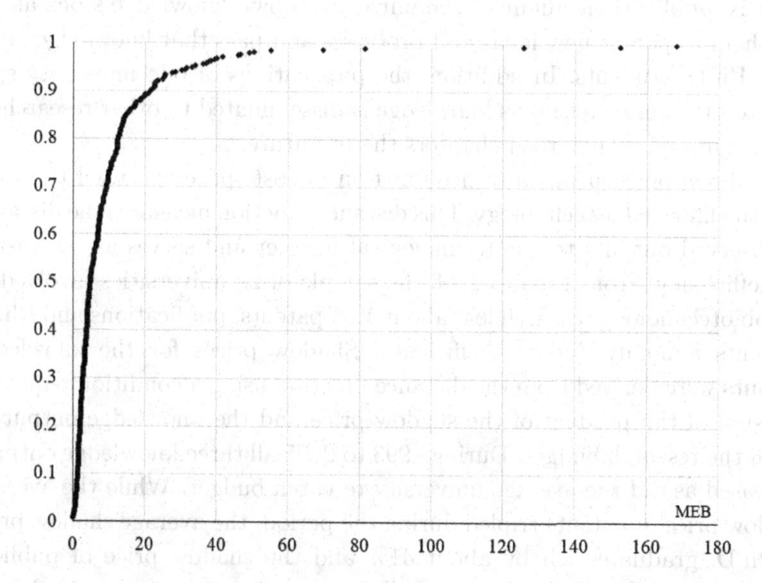

Fig. 11.4: Cumulative Distribution Function of the Marginal External Benefit of Publications

1993, down to $6.39 million in 1999 to a high of $21.37 million in 2005. Several outliers appear to be skewing the data as shown in Figure 11.4, which gives the cumulative distribution function of the pooled estimates of the MEB received by each university. The last column of Table 11.6 reports the proportion of the budget consisting of the MEB. These values average 0.027 and range from 0.019 in 2001 to 0.041 in 2005. Thus, at the margin, spillover publications help each university hold costs down by 2.7% of the average budget.

11.7 Conclusions

The production of knowledge outputs by universities is an important driver of productivity growth (Adams, 1990; Elnasri and Fox, 2017). This chapter constructed a network model for university knowledge outputs — publications, patents and Ph.D. students — in the area of nanobiotechnology. To produce the knowledge outputs, each university has a research budget which they use to hire researchers, furnish laboratories and buy equipment. The publications that a university produces in one period is an intermediate product that becomes an input to the subsequent period. That is, publications augment the university's own knowledge stock allowing them to patent new ideas and processes and pass that knowledge on to their Ph.D. students. In addition, the publications of one university spill over to other universities as knowledge is disseminated to other researchers and engineers as they read chapters the literature.

A directional output distance function in cost space was used to represent the knowledge technology. This distance function measures the distance of observed outputs to the technological frontier and serves as a measure of inefficiency. From 1993 to 2005 the sample of 29 universities involved in nanobiotechnology research lost about 1.65 patents, publications and Ph.D. students annually due to inefficiency. Shadow prices for the knowledge outputs were derived from the distance function using a condition requiring the sum of the product of the shadow price and the knowledge output to equal the research budget. During 1993 to 2005 all three knowledge outputs increased as did the average university research budget. While the average shadow price of patents tripled during the period, the average shadow price of Ph.D. graduates fell by about 41% and the shadow price of publications fell by 63%. The spillover benefit that each university received from the publications of other universities averaged about 2.7% of the university budget. That is, without the publications of other universities, each university would have needed an additional 2.7% in research expenditures to produce the same knowledge outputs.

Appendix

In the first section we introduce and briefly discuss the axioms that will be imposed on the technology. In the following section we list similar axioms for the indirect technologies. (see also Shephard, 1970; Färe and Primont, 1995).

Recall that $x \in \Re_+^N$ denotes an input vector and $y \in \Re_+^M$ an output vector. Moreover, in Chapter 1, we introduced representations of the black box technology

(i) $T = \{(x, y) : x \text{ can produce } y\}$
(ii) $P(x) = \{y : (x, y) \in T\}$
(iii) $L(y) = \{x : (x, y) \in T\}$.

We also proved that

$$(x, y) \in T \Leftrightarrow x \in L(y) \Leftrightarrow y \in P(x).$$

A. The Black Box Axioms

We start by introducing two conditions with respect to inactivity.

A.1 $(0, 0) \in T$.

A.2 $0 \in P(x)$ for all $x \in \Re_+^N$.

Since $0 \in \Re_+^N$, A.2 $\Rightarrow$ A.1.

A.1 says that firms may choose to use no inputs, which in turn would yield no outputs. This implies that T is a non-empty set.

A.2 says that the firm may produce zero outputs even if inputs are positive, i.e., they may choose not to produce outputs and 'waste' inputs.

For duality theory, convexity is a fundamental condition. Each of the three production sets may be assumed to be convex, although this will affect the resulting returns to scale in some cases. Hence we require

A.3 $(x, y), (x', y') \in T, 0 \leqq \lambda \leqq 1 \Rightarrow (1 - \lambda)(x, y) + \lambda(x', y') \in T.$

A.3 models convexity of the technology set, whereas A.3 and A.1 together imply non-increasing returns to scale (NIRS):

Let (x', y') and $(0, 0) \in T$, then $(\lambda x', \lambda y') \in T$ for $0 \leqq \lambda \leqq 1$, modeling NIRS.

Moreover, in A.3 if we take $x = x'$ then the output set is also convex, i.e.,

A.4 $(1 - \lambda)y + \lambda y' \in P(x), 0 \leqq \lambda \leqq 1.$

And if we take $y = y'$, the input set is convex, i.e.,

A.5 $(1 - \lambda)x + \lambda x' \in L(y).$

Note that A.4 does not imply A.3 nor does A.5. This is demonstrated in Figure A.1.

In the figure, for each $x \in \Re_+, P(x)$ is convex and for each $y \in \Re_+, L(y)$ is convex, however T is not convex as shown.

Convexity captures the intuitive idea that if extremes are feasible, so are the averages of those extremes.

Next we turn to conditions on the boundaries of these sets, which includes the notion of a closed set, i.e., one which includes its boundary points. This is an essential condition for seeking objectives of maximization or minimization over the set. As with convexity, each of our three production sets may be closed.

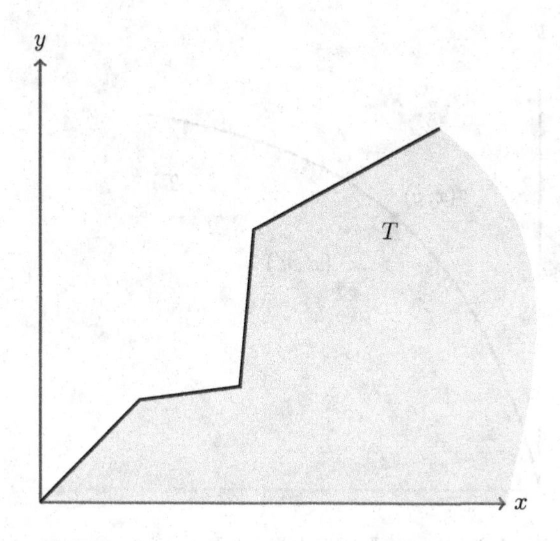

Fig. A.1: $P(x)$, $L(y)$ Convex but not T

A.6 T is closed, i.e., $[(x^n, y^n) \in T$ for all n and $(x^n, y^n) \to (x^o, y^o)$ as $n \to \infty] \Rightarrow (x^o, y^o) \in T$.

A.6 models closedness of the technology set. If we take $x^n = x$ for all n, closedness of the output set is modelled

A.7 $[y^n \in P(x), y^n \to y^o] \Rightarrow y^o \in P(x)$.

If $y^n = y$ for all n, the input set is closed:

A.8 $[\, x^n \in L(y), x^n \to x^o] \Rightarrow x^o \in L(y)$.

Thus, A.6 $\Rightarrow$ A.7 and A.8 but the converse is not true.

We next turn to axioms concerning the disposability of inputs and outputs. We say that the technology set is monotonic or equivalently that inputs and outputs are strongly (freely) disposable if

A.9 $(x, y) \in T$ and $x' \geqq x, y' \leqq y \Rightarrow (x', y') \in T$.

Figure A.2 illustrates.

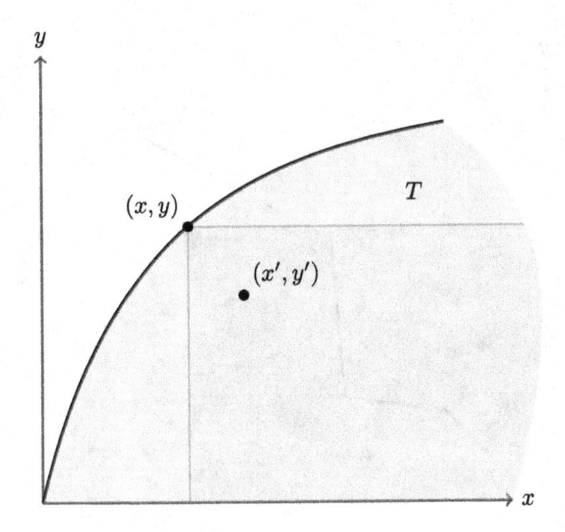

Fig. A.2: Strong Disposability of Inputs and Outputs

In the figure, (x, y) belongs to the technology set T and x' is not less than x and y' not larger than y. As shown, (x', y') also belongs to T, that is x' can produce y'.

If we take $x' = x$, then A.9 implies that outputs (alone) are strongly disposable, i.e.,

A.10 $y \in P(x)$ and $y' \leqq y$ then $y' \in P(x)$.

Similarly, if we take $y' = y$, then A.9 implies that inputs (alone) are strongly disposable, i.e.,

A.11 $x \in L(y)$ and $x' \geqq x$ then $x' \in L(y)$.

Thus, one may 'waste' or freely dispose of inputs.

With respect to duality theory, disposability has implications for the range of prices required for duality to hold. Specifically, strong disposability of outputs implies that output prices need only be non-negative to recover the output set from its dual — the revenue function. Similar conditions apply for recovering the technology set from the profit function and the input set from the cost function.

This non-negativity arises because strong disposability prevents the various boundaries of the sets from atypical curvature, e.g., backward bending input isoquants or positively sloped segments of the output set boundary. Such atypical curvature may be useful for modeling congestion on the input side or costly disposal of undesirable by-products on the output side. For this reason we include two weaker disposability conditions

A.10W $y \in P(x), 0 \leqq \lambda \leqq 1 \Rightarrow \lambda y \in P(x)$.

A.10W models what we call weak disposability of outputs. Note that if both A.2 $0 \in P(x)$ for all $x \in \Re^N_+$ and A.4 $P(x)$ is convex hold, then outputs are weakly disposable, i.e., proportional contractions of all outputs simultaneously are feasible.[1] To verify this take $y = 0$ then with A.2 and A.4 we have

$$\text{for } 0 \leqq \lambda \leqq 1, (1-\lambda)0 + \lambda y' = \lambda y' \in P(x), \tag{A.1}$$

i.e., A.10W holds.

We say that inputs are weakly disposable if

A.11W $x \in L(y), \lambda \geqq 1 \Rightarrow \lambda x \in L(y)$.

The following production function is an example that satisfies A.11W but not A.11.

$y = x_1^\alpha \cdot (x_2 - ax_1)^{1-\alpha}$ if $(x_2 - ax_1) \geqq 0$,

$y = 0$ otherwise,

Figure A.3 illustrates.

No output is produced in the region where $(x_2 - ax_1) \leqq 0$ and output is positive where $(x_2 - ax_1) > 0$. The figure illustrates that if output is positive, then disposing of (increasing) x_1 will eventually result in output falling to zero, which is characteristic of a congesting input.

[1] But it does not necessarily follow that reductions in individual outputs are feasible.

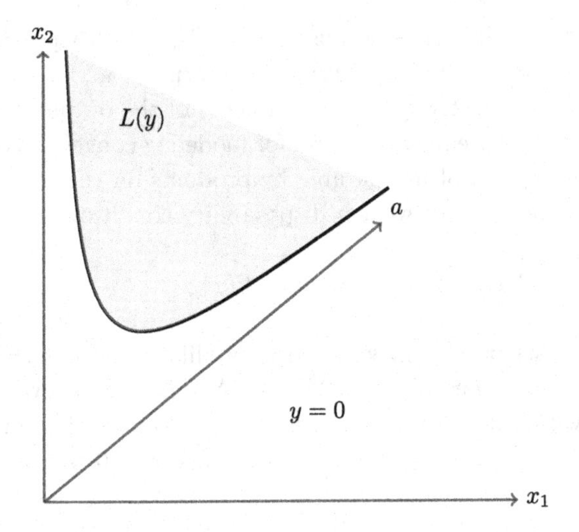

Fig. A.3: Weak Disposability of Inputs

The notion of scarcity is fundamental to our models of production. Here we assume that the output set is bounded for each input vector $x \in \Re^N_+$:

A.12 $P(x)$ is bounded for each $x \in \Re^N_+$.

This means that if inputs are finite, so too are the outputs that input produces. In addition we say that there is 'no free lunch':

A.13 $(x, y) \in T, x = 0 \Rightarrow y = 0$,

which says that if inputs are zero, no output can be produced. The contrapositive statement

$$(x, y) \in T, y \geq 0 \Rightarrow x \geq 0, \tag{A.2}$$

shows that 'positive' output requires 'positive' inputs. An additional interpretation of A.13 is that inputs are essential for producing output.

Earlier we said that production technology exhibits NIRS if

A.14 $(x, y) \in T$ and $0 \leqq \lambda \leqq 1 \Rightarrow (\lambda x, \lambda y) \in T$.

Technology may also exhibit constant-returns-to-scale (CRS) if

A.15 $(x, y) \in T$ and $\lambda \geqq 0 \Rightarrow (\lambda x, \lambda y) \in T$,

and non-decreasing returns to scale (NDRS) if

A.16 $(x, y) \in T$ and $\lambda \geqq 1 \Rightarrow (\lambda x, \lambda y) \in T$.

Clearly from the condition that

$$(x, y) \in T \Leftrightarrow x \in L(y) \Leftrightarrow y \in P(x), \tag{A.3}$$

one may define these various returns to scale on the equivalent input and output sets.

B. Cost and Revenue Indirect Technologies

Denote input prices by $w = (w_1, \ldots, w_N) \in \Re_+^N$ and target cost or allowed budget by $c \in \Re_+$. The cost indirect output set for given (w, c) is

$$IP(w/c) = \{y : y \in P(x), wx \leqq c\}. \tag{B.1}$$

This output set (also referred to as output correspondence) consists of all feasible output vectors $y \in P(x)$ that cost no more than c to produce, i.e., $wx \leqq c$. By homogeneity of degree $+1$ of the budget constraint we may write

$$wx \leqq c, \text{ as } \frac{w}{c} x \leqq 1,$$

given that $c > 0$, which we impose in the rest of this document. If in addition we assume that the inactivity condition A.2 holds, then it follows that

IP.1 $0 \in IP(w/c)$.

To verify this, note that A.2 states that $0 \in P(x)$, for all $x \in \Re_+^N$. Since $0 \in \Re_+^N$, it follows that $w \times 0 \leqq c$, verifying IP.1.

Next, we turn to the convexity axiom A.3, and show that it holds for the indirect technology as well.

Let A.3 hold, then for

$$y \in P(x), y' \in P(x') \text{ and for } 0 \leqq \lambda \leqq 1,$$

it follows that

$$(1-\lambda)y + \lambda y' \in P((1-\lambda)x + \lambda x'). \tag{B.2}$$

Now let $y, y' \in IP(w/c)$, then $y \in P(x)$ and $y' \in P(x')$, with $wx \leq c$ and $wx' \leqq c$. By the convexity relationship above we have

$$(1-\lambda)y + \lambda y' \in P((1-\lambda)x + \lambda x') \text{ and } \lambda wx + (1-\lambda)wx' \leqq c, \tag{B.3}$$

proving convexity of $IP(w/c)$.

IP.2 If T is convex, $IP(w/c)$ is convex.

The next two conditions on the indirect technology are

IP.3 If $(w/c) > 0, IP(w/c)$ is bounded.

IP.4 If $(w/c) > 0, IP(w/c)$ is closed. (for proofs, see (Färe and Grosskopf, 1994, p. 16)).

With respect to disposability we have

IP.5 $(w/c)' \geqq (w/c) \Leftrightarrow IP((w/c)') \subseteq IP(w/c)$.

IP.6 If A.10 holds, then $y' \leqq y \in IP(w/c) \Leftrightarrow y' \in IP(w/c)$.

Bibliography

Aczél, J. (1966). *Lectures on Functional Equations and Their Applications*, Vol. 19 (Academic press, New York).

Adams, J. D. (1990). Fundamental stocks of knowledge and productivity growth, *Journal of Political Economy* **98**, 4, pp. 673–702.

Aigner, D. J. and Chu, S.-F. (1968). On estimating the industry production function, *The American Economic Review* **58**, 4, pp. 826–839.

Aigner, D., Lovell, C. K., and Schmidt, P. (1977). Formulation and estimation of stochastic frontier production function models, *Journal of Econometrics* **6**, 1, pp. 21–37.

Allais, M. (1943). *A la recherche d'une discipline économique: Première partie économie pure* (Impr. Ateliers Industria).

Allen, F., Carletti, E., and Marquez, R. (2015). Deposits and bank capital structure, *Journal of Financial Economics* **118**, 3, pp. 601–619.

Atkinson, S. E. and Tsionas, M. G. (2016). Directional distance functions: Optimal endogenous directions, *Journal of Econometrics* **190**, 2, pp. 301–314.

Azoulay, P., Ding, W., and Stuart, T. (2009). The impact of academic patenting on the rate, quality and direction of (public) research output, *The Journal of Industrial Economics* **57**, 4, pp. 637–676.

Baker, M. and Wurgler, J. (2013). Do strict capital requirements raise the cost of capital? Banking regulation and the low risk anomaly, Technical Report, National Bureau of Economic Research.

Barnes, M. L. and Lopez, J. A. (2006). Alternative measures of the Federal Reserve Banks' cost of equity capital, *Journal of Banking & Finance* **30**, 6, pp. 1687–1711.

Belotti, F., Daidone, S., Ilardi, G., and Atella, V. (2013). Stochastic frontier analysis using Stata, *The Stata Journal* **13**, 4, pp. 719–758.

Berger, A. N. (2007). International comparisons of banking efficiency, *Financial Markets, Institutions & Instruments* **16**, 3, pp. 119–144.

Berger, A. N. and Humphrey, D. B. (1997). Efficiency of financial institutions: International survey and directions for future research, *European Journal of Operational Research* **98**, 2, pp. 175–212.

Berger, A. N. and Mester, L. J. (2003). Explaining the dramatic changes in performance of US banks: Technological change, deregulation, and dynamic changes in competition, *Journal of Financial Intermediation* **12**, 1, pp. 57–95.

Bobzin, H. (1998). Indivisibilities: Micro theory with respect to indivisible goods and factors. Heidelberg: Physica-Verlag.

Camillo, C. A. (2012). Divine providence: The 2011 flood in the mississippi river and tributaries project, US Army Corps of Engineers.

Case, F. (2011). Nanotech decade, *Chemistry World* **8**, 3, pp. 46–49.

Chambers, R. G. (1988). *Applied Production Analysis: A Dual Approach* (Cambridge University Press, Cambridge).

Chambers, R. G. (1998). Input and output indicators, in *Index Numbers: Essays in Honour of Sten Malmquist* (Springer) is Dordrecht, pp. 241–271.

Chambers, R. G. (2002). Exact nonradial input, output, and productivity measurement, *Economic Theory* **20**, 4, pp. 751–765.

Chambers, R. G., Chung, Y., and Färe, R. (1996). Benefit and distance functions, *Journal of Economic Theory* **70**, 2, pp. 407–419.

Chambers, R. G., Chung, Y., and Färe, R. (1998). Profit, directional distance functions, and Nerlovian efficiency, *Journal of Optimization Theory and Applications* **98**, 2, pp. 351–364.

Chambers, R. G. and Färe, R. (2004). Additive decomposition of profit efficiency, *Economics Letters* **84**, 3, pp. 329–334.

Christensen, L. R., Jorgenson, D. W., and Lau, L. J. (1971). Conjugate duality and the transcendental logarithmic production function, *Econometrica* **39**, 4, pp. 255–256.

Coelli, T. and Perelman, S. (1996). Efficiency measurement, multiple-output technologies and distance functions: With application to European railways. Crepp WP 96/05, Centre de Recherche en Économie Publique et de la Population (CREP), Liége, Belgium.

Coelli, T. and Perelman, S. (2000). Technical efficiency of European railways: A distance function approach, *Applied Economics* **32**, 15, pp. 1967–1976.

de Campos, T. C. (2015). The idea of patents vs. the idea of university, *The New Bioethics* **21**, 2, pp. 164–176.

Denny, M. (1974). The relationship between functional forms for the production system, *The Canadian Journal of Economics* **7**, 1, pp. 21–31.

Diewert, W. E. and Shimizu, C. (2015). A conceptual framework for commercial property price indexes, *Journal of Statistical Science and Application*, **3**, 9–10, pp. 131–152.

Diewert, W. E. (1976). Exact and superlative index numbers, *Journal of Econometrics* **4**, 2, pp. 115–145.

Diewert, W. E. (2002). The quadratic approximation lemma and decompositions of superlative indexes, *Journal of Economic and Social Measurement* **28**, 1, 2, pp. 63–88.

Diewert, W. E. (2003). Hedonic regressions. A consumer theory approach, in *Scanner Data and Price Indexes* (University of Chicago Press), pp. 317–348.

Diewert, W. E. (2011). Alternative approaches to measuring house price inflation, Tech. rep., Discussion Paper 10-10, Department of Economics, The University of British Columbia, Vancouver, Canada.

Elnasri, A. and Fox, K. J. (2017). The contribution of research and innovation to productivity, *Journal of Productivity Analysis* **47**, 3, pp. 291–308.

Fabrizio, K. R. and Di Minin, A. (2008). Commercializing the laboratory: Faculty patenting and the open science environment, *Research Policy* **37**, 5, pp. 914–931.

Färe, R. and Grosskopf, S. (1994). *Cost and Revenue Constrained Production* (Springer Verlag, Berlin).

Färe, R. and Grosskopf, S. (1996). *Intertemporal Production Frontiers: With Dynamic DEA* (Kluwer Academic Publishers, Boston).

Färe, R., Grosskopf, S., and Lovell, C. K. (1985). *The Measurement of Efficiency of Production*, Vol. 6 (Springer Science & Business Media).

Färe, R., Grosskopf, S., Lovell, C. K., and Yaisawarng, S. (1993). Derivation of shadow prices for undesirable outputs: A distance function approach, *The Review of Economics and Statistics* **75**, 2, pp. 374–380.

Färe, R., Grosskopf, S., Margaritis, D., and Weber, W. L. (2012). Technological change and timing reductions in greenhouse gas emissions, *Journal of Productivity Analysis* **37**, 3, pp. 205–216.

Färe, R., Grosskopf, S., Noh, D.-W., and Weber, W. (2005). Characteristics of a polluting technology: Theory and practice, *Journal of Econometrics* **126**, 2, pp. 469–492.

Färe, R., Grosskopf, S., and Weber, W. L. (2001). Shadow prices of Missouri public conservation land, *Public Finance Review* **29**, 6, pp. 444–460.

Färe, R., Grosskopf, S., and Weber, W. L. (2016). Pricing nonmarketed outputs with an application to community colleges, *Public Finance Review* **44**, 2, pp. 197–219.

Färe, R., Grosskopf, S., and Whittaker, G. (2014). Network DEA II, in *Data Envelopment Analysis* (Springer), pp. 307–327.

Färe, R. and Lundberg, A. (2006). Parameterizing the shortage function, mimeo. Department of Economics, Oregon State University.

Färe, R., Martins-Filho, C., and Vardanyan, M. (2010). On functional form representation of multi-output production technologies, *Journal of Productivity Analysis* **33**, 2, pp. 81–96.

Färe, R. and Primont, D. (1995). *Multi-output Production and Duality: Theory and Applications* (Kluwer Academic Publishers, Boston).

Färe, R. and Sung, K. J. (1986). On second-order Taylor's-series approximation and linear homogeneity, *Aequationes Mathematicae* **30**, 1, pp. 180–186.

Fethi, M. D. and Pasiouras, F. (2010). Assessing bank efficiency and performance with operational research and artificial intelligence techniques: A survey, *European Journal of Operational Research* **204**, 2, pp. 189–198.

Fleming, W. (1977). *Functions of Several Variables* (Springer Verlag, Heidelberg, New York).

Foltz, J. D., Barham, B. L., and Kim, K. (2007). Synergies or trade-offs in university life sciences research, *American Journal of Agricultural Economics* **89**, 2, pp. 353–367.

Foltz, J. D., Kim, K., and Barham, B. (2003). A dynamic analysis of university agricultural biotechnology patent production, *American Journal of Agricultural Economics* **85**, 1, pp. 187–197.

Fukuyama, H. and Weber, W. L. (2008). Japanese banking inefficiency and shadow pricing, *Mathematical and Computer Modelling* **48**, 11–12, pp. 1854–1867.

Fukuyama, H., Weber, W. L., and Xia, Y. (2015). Time substitution and network effects with an application to nanobiotechnology policy for US universities, *Omega* **60**, pp. 34–44.

Good, D. H., Sickles, R. C., and Weiher, J. C. (2008). A hedonic price index for airline travel, *Review of Income and Wealth* **54**, 3, pp. 438–465.

Green, E. J., Lopez, J. A., and Wang, Z. (2003). Formulating the imputed cost of equity capital for priced services at Federal Reserve Banks, *Economic Policy Review* **9**, 3, pp. 55–81.

Heimlich, R. E., Wiebe, K. D., Claassen, R., Gadsby, D., and House, R. M. (1998). Wetlands and agriculture: Private interests and public benefits, *Agricultural Economics Report* **765**, p. 104.

Hoyt, W. G. and Langbein, W. B. (1955). *Floods* (Princeton University Press).

Hudgins, L. B. and Primont, D. (2007). Derivative properties of directional technology distance functions, in *Aggregation, Efficiency, and Measurement* (Springer), pp. 31–43.

Hughes, J. P., Mester, L. J., and Moon, C.-G. (2001). Are scale economies in banking elusive or illusive? Evidence obtained by incorporating capital structure and risk-taking into models of bank production, *Journal of Banking & Finance* **25**, 12, pp. 2169–2208.

Kao, C. (2013). Dynamic data envelopment analysis: A relational analysis, *European Journal of Operational Research* **227**, 2, pp. 325–330.

Kao, C. (2014). Network data envelopment analysis: A review, *European Journal of Operational Research* **239**, 1, pp. 1–16.

King, M. R. (2009). The cost of equity for global banks: A CAPM perspective from 1990 to 2009, *BIS Quarterly Review*, pp. 59–73.

Koutsomanoli-Filippaki, A., Margaritis, D., and Staikouras, C. (2009). Efficiency and productivity growth in the banking industry of Central and Eastern Europe, *Journal of Banking & Finance* **33**, 3, pp. 557–567.

Ledwin, J. and Roberts, A. (2000). St. Johns Bayou and New Madrid Floodway Project: East Priairie Phase. US Fish and Wildlife Service, Ecological Services Field Office, Columbia, Missouri.

Lovell, C. K., Travers, P., Richardson, S., and Wood, L. (1994). Resources and functionings: A new view of inequality in Australia, in *Models and Measurement of Welfare and Inequality* (Springer), pp. 787–807.

Luenberger, D. G. (1992). Benefit functions and duality, *Journal of Mathematical Economics* **21**, 5, pp. 461–481.

Luenberger, D. G. (1995). *Microeconomic Theory* (McGraw-Hill College).

Mas-Colell, A., Whinston, M. D., and Green, J. R. (1995). *Microeconomic Theory*, Vol. 1 (Oxford University Press, New York).

McMillen, D. P. (2003). The return of centralization to Chicago: Using repeat sales to identify changes in house price distance gradients, *Regional Science and Urban Economics* **33**, 3, pp. 287–304.

Murty, S., Russell, R. R., and Levkoff, S. (2012). On modeling pollution-generating technologies, *Journal of Environmental Economics and Management* **64**, 1, pp. 117–135.

Olson, K. R. and Morton, L. W. (2013). Impacts of 2011 len small levee breach on private and public Illinois lands, *Journal of Soil and Water Conservation* **68**, 4, pp. 89A–95A.

Roco, M. (2016). National nanotechnology investment in the FY 2016 budget, in *The President's FY 2016 Budget* (American Society of Mechanical Engineers).

Sealey, C. W. and Lindley, J. T. (1977). Inputs, outputs, and a theory of production and cost at depository financial institutions, *The Journal of Finance* **32**, 4, pp. 1251–1266.

Shephard, R. W. (1953). *Cost and Production Functions* (Princeton University Press, Princeton).

Shephard, R. W. (1970). *Theory of Cost and Production Functions* (Princeton University Press, Princeton).

Shephard, R. W. (1974). *Indirect Production Functions* (Anton Hain, Cambridge).

Thorsnes, P. (1997). Consistent estimates of the elasticity of substitution between land and non-land inputs in the production of housing, *Journal of Urban Economics* **42**, 1, pp. 98–108.

Weber, W. L. (2015). On the economic value of wetlands in the St. John's Bayou-New Madrid Floodway, Southeast Missouri State University.

Weber, W. L. and Xia, Y. (2011). The productivity of nanobiotechnology research and education in US universities, *American Journal of Agricultural Economics* **93**, 4, pp. 1151–1167.

Weyman-Jones, T. (2016). Efficiency, competition and the shadow price of capital, in *The Handbook of Post Crisis Financial Modeling* (Springer), pp. 147–167.

Author Index

I

J

K

L

M

P

R

S

T

V

W

X

Y

Subject Index

World Scientific–Now Publishers Series in Business

(Continuation of series card page)

Vol. 11 *Global Sourcing of Services: Strategies, Issues and Challenges*
edited by Shailendra C. Jain Palvia and Prashant Palvia

Vol. 10 *Cross-Functional Inventory Research*
edited by Srinagesh Gavirneni

Vol. 9 *The First Great Financial Crisis of the 21st Century: A Retrospective*
edited by George G. Kaufman and James R. Barth

Vol. 8 *Advances in Data Envelopment Analysis*
by Rolf Färe, Shawna Grosskopf and Dimitris Margaritis

Vol. 7 *Diagnostics for a Globalized World*
by Sten Thore and Ruzanna Tarverdyan

Vol. 6 *Superpower, China? Historicizing Beijing's New Narratives of Leadership and East Asia's Response Thereto*
by Niv Horesh, Hyun Jin Kim and Peter Mauch

Vol. 5 *Contingent Convertibles [CoCos]: A Potent Instrument for Financial Reform*
by George M. von Furstenberg

Vol. 4 *The Analysis of Competition Policy and Sectoral Regulation*
edited by Martin Peitz and Yossi Spiegel

Vol. 3 *The History of Marketing Science*
edited by Russell S. Winer and Scott A. Neslin

Vol. 2 *Dodd–Frank Wall Street Reform and Consumer Protection Act: Purpose, Critique, Implementation Status and Policy Issues*
edited by Douglas D. Evanoff and William F. Moeller

Vol. 1 *Games and Dynamic Games*
by Alain Haurie, Jacek B. Krawczyk and Georges Zaccour

World Scientific-Now Publishers Series in Business

[illegible]

Printed in the United States
by Bookmasters

Printed in the United States
By Bookmasters